"In a book rich with wisdom and insight, Darr... ____ ___ sonal and spiritual development that suits the needs of modern life. If you follow its guidelines, you will surely experience greater contentment and fulfillment."

—STEVE TAYLOR, Ph.D., author of *The Leap* and *Spiritual Science* and featured in Watkins' list of the 100 most spiritually influential people

"*Living a Life of Harmony* can help us all do just that. It is simple to follow, down-to-earth, and practical, with many suggestions that can help us bring our lives more in line with our spiritual values. Darren has been influenced by the teachings of Buddha, yoga, and, from modern times, Eckhart Tolle, but you don't have to be acquainted with any of them to understand and apply his ideas. This book is absolutely for and of its time, bringing perennial principles to life for the twenty-first century."

— SARAH RYAN, yoga teacher

"*Living a Life of Harmony* is a resource I would encourage people with addiction issues to study. Someone with an addiction will often overcomplicate and ruminate to a level far removed from the reality of their situation. Recovery is therefore essentially a correction of views. In this book they will see and appreciate the practical maxim, 'Do the right things and the right things will follow.' They will gain insight into the reasons why we change our conditions, beyond the need to end personal suffering. Over time, if we follow the guidelines proposed by Darren, we can bring ourselves into alignment with the way things really are and see and feel the harmony that was always there."

— DENNIS WAREING, substance misuse worker

"*Living a Life of Harmony* is a handbook for everyday living! Darren explains how life is one big universal process, which he calls 'The Process,' and how everything is connected. While reading this book, I felt as if I was being gently and lovingly walked through each part of The Process, step-by-step, at my own pace. I felt empowered and confident in the choices I was making, as I had a structured way of assessing each choice so that it would have a positive effect, not only on myself but on those around me. This book has transformed how I approach my everyday life and I highly recommend it."

— LOUISE FRENCH, healer

LIVING A LIFE OF HARMONY

Seven Guidelines for Cultivating Peace and Kindness

DARREN COCKBURN

FINDHORN PRESS

Findhorn Press
One Park Street
Rochester, Vermont 05767
www.findhornpress.com

Text stock is SFI certified

Findhorn Press is a division of Inner Traditions International

Disclaimer
The information in this book is given in good faith and is neither intended to diagnose
any physical or mental condition nor to serve as a substitute for informed medical
advice or care. The author of this book does not dispense medical advice nor prescribe
the use of any food or technique as a form of treatment for medical problems. Please
contact your health professional for medical advice and treatment. Neither author nor
publisher can be held liable by any person for any loss or damage whatsoever which may
arise directly or indirectly from the use of this book or any of the information therein.

Cataloging-in-Publication Data for this title is available from the Library of Congress

ISBN 978-1-62055-890-4 (print)
ISBN 978-1-62055-891-1 (ebook)

Printed and bound in the United States by Lake Book Manufacturing, Inc.
The text stock is SFI certified. The Sustainable Forestry Initiative® program promotes
sustainable forest management.

10 9 8 7 6 5 4 3 2 1

Edited by Michael Hawkins
Text design, layout and diagrams by Damian Keenan
This book was typeset in Adobe Garamond Pro and Calluna Sans with Bernhard
Modern used as a display typeface.

To send correspondence to the author of this book, mail a first-class letter to the
author c/o Inner Traditions • Bear & Company, One Park Street, Rochester, VT
05767, USA, and we will forward the communication, or contact the author directly
at **www.darrencockburn.com**

Contents

Introduction

HAVE YOU EVER asked yourself why things happen? Why you're here on earth, and what role you play in it all? How can you remain peaceful, and live a life of harmony? In this book I'll be guiding you to explore and answer these intriguing questions. You can look at them from a spiritual or scientific standpoint. When spiritual teachings align with science and logic, you've found the truth. For example, Buddhist teachings talk about things being conditioned. Switch on the kettle and your water heats up – it's logical. Cause and effect can also be proved scientifically by examining what's going on at a molecular level. Then there are spiritual teachings that science is still to prove. Many religions state that God creates and destroys everything. That's not been proven scientifically. In these instances, you decide for yourself whether to believe.

I haven't written this book to convince you that God is real or isn't real. It's not my place to do that. I'll be discussing the wider area of spirituality rather than specific belief systems or religions. The teachings in this book are beneficial regardless of whether you believe in a higher power. At various points I'll claim that some things are true that cannot be proven with logic or science. You can take or leave these things. It's your call. You are in charge of what you believe. Hear me out though. Give me the time to explain what I know, and see where it leads you...

The first thing to get your head around is that there's one big universal process. What I call "The Process." Everything's connected. This causes that to happen. That causes this to happen. Cause and effect. All the pleasant stuff. All the unpleasant stuff. All the neutral stuff. All the bodily sensations, thoughts, and feelings, of the approximately eight billion people that live on this planet are part of The Process. All of nature is part of The Process. It goes wider than that. The billions of galaxies, planets, and every atom that resides on them are all part of The Process. It's HUGE!

Through a series of explanations, examples, and techniques, I'll help you gain a deeper understanding and acceptance of this universal process. To keep things simple, our focus will be on what happens here on earth, rather than the whole universe! You'll be ultimately placed to observe and accept everything, leaving you feeling empowered, peaceful, confident and stress free. Your new way of using your mind will give you the option to act wisely, regardless of the conditions you face.

Some religions and philosophies encourage people to work towards freeing themselves from this process of cause and effect. Buddhism and Yoga are good examples of this. They refer to cause and effect on a personal level as karma. This is part of The Process. Some teachings claim that you can transcend into pure emptiness or the source creator that sits behind The Process. At that point, it's claimed that you're no longer a part of The Process, and you become the space within which it unfolds. Names given to this state of being include awakening and enlightenment. In Buddhist philosophy, The Buddha is claimed to have achieved this state. Christians may tell you that Jesus was enlightened. Having a goal of enlightenment is fully compatible with the teachings we'll be exploring within this book, as they're aligned with the truth of all quality religions and philosophies. It's fine if you don't believe in enlightenment. This book will help you navigate The Process, and live a life of harmony.

Over the centuries, countless religions and philosophies have produced wonderful lists that guide their followers to act ethically and in accordance with The Process. People are advised not to steal, to speak truthfully, not to cause harm, to be loyal to their partners and so on. I've studied and practiced some of these lists and they've been extremely helpful. That said, it's challenging to understand and apply them these days, given that they were written so long ago. In *Living a Life of Harmony*, I'm introducing a fresh and evolutionary set of guidelines that are simple to understand and practical now, in the twenty-first century. The Guidelines are based on common sense and recommended in teachings from some of the world's great religions and philosophies. There is only one truth. What's new and fresh about this book is the orchestration of these teachings into the seven guidelines. I'm going to present these guidelines in a way that you can understand and apply them, in your present life situation. This will provide you with a compass to guide you through The Process. Here are "The Guidelines" presented in list and diagrammatic forms:

1. Honor the body.
2. Be present, bringing awareness and acceptance into every moment.
3. Act with kindness, considering everyone and everything.

4. Understand the truth, communicating it selectively and skillfully.
5. Do only what needs to be done.
6. Harmoniously obtain and retain only what you need.
7. Apply The Guidelines to your digital device usage.

The Seven Guidelines

The Guidelines

These simple guidelines, offer far-reaching benefits for those who understand and follow them. I'll be explaining what each of these guidelines really means, and providing examples of everyday applications based on real life experience. I'll also explain what the guidelines do not mean, to help avoid any misinterpretation. You'll be offered techniques and pointers you can use that will help you understand and live by The Guidelines. The ultimate result for you, should you choose to follow them, will be a peaceful mind and a life of harmony, within The Process. I cannot predict or guarantee what will happen to the content of your life though. The Guidelines are not there to help you achieve this or that. Paradoxically though, if you do apply them, you're more likely to set and achieve goals that are aligned with what's needed; and also enjoy the process of achieving those goals. Following The Guidelines will mean changes for you. Possibly big changes. I appreciate it's a big ask to take the leap.

For most, it takes time and effort to understand and apply The Guidelines consistently. We create a practice for ourselves, work diligently with it, and over time we observe the fruits. The fruits then give us more faith in The Guidelines which creates a positive chain reaction. You will start to realize benefits quickly and this will reassure you that you're on the right path. The time and effort required to master The Guidelines varies from person to person. The Process created you. And now you, its creation, are becoming aware of the creator. The Process is also becoming more aware of itself through its own creation.

The Guidelines are compatible with any quality religion or philosophy. By 'quality' I'm referring to a religion or philosophy that presents the truth. If this is the case, The Guidelines here and any pointers offered in the religion or philosophy will align beautifully. If you already have a spiritual practice then wonderful. You're invited to read on and learn more. If you don't have a spiritual practice, that's fine. You're invited to make the guidance in this book your core spiritual practice.

I use the words *aligned* and *misaligned* throughout the book. Unless stated otherwise, I'm referring to alignment and misalignment with The Guidelines and The Process. When people misunderstand The Guidelines, they may apply them in a way that's misaligned and cause harm. This is why I place great emphasis on reading the book carefully and reflecting upon what each guideline really means. I use the words *aligned* and *skillful* interchangeably. Also, I use the words *misaligned* and *unskillful* interchangeably.

Chapter One explains The Process in more detail and offers practices to help you better understand it. Following on, in Chapter Two, context and background is provided on the full set of guidelines to help you build faith, motivation and confidence in their application. Then, from Chapter Three, guidelines are presented in turn with their own dedicated chapters. Each guideline chapter provides a thorough explanation of what the guideline really means, real life examples of its application and practical tips for following it. The final chapter talks through how to structure, prioritize, and organize your practice, across all seven guidelines. It also collates many opportunities for practicing The Guidelines in everyday life into an accessible tabular format. Initially, it will be helpful for you to work through the book from cover to cover. Subsequently, you can refer to the individual chapters as required. The book doubles up as a handy reference guide for your ongoing practice.

At the end of each chapter, you'll find a section labelled 'Points for Reflection,' which repeats a short list of some of the key elements from the main text. To support your learning, I advise you to reflect on each point in the context of your own personal situation and understanding. This should be undertaken slowly and mindfully, followed by a pause for reflection after each point. In addition, it can help to reflect with friends or in a group. Refrain from using the points for reflection as an alternative to reading the main content of the chapters. The main content and key points must be used together, to provide the context of the teachings and the greatest opportunity to reflect and learn. You may also return to the key points from each chapter as a reference point in the future.

Personal journey

Before we move into the core chapters of the book, let me take an opportunity to share a little about my personal journey and how this book came about. When I was in my early twenties I struggled with work-life balance, anxiety and alcohol addiction. I achieved quite a lot, whilst being stressed most of the time and drinking most days. It felt like my mind was out of control and I had little self-awareness. Relationships were fraught and difficult to maintain. My mind was so busy thinking about 'me,' I was unable to empathize with how others were feeling. Thankfully there was enough awareness in me to realize that my frantic mind needed taming, and I needed to become more peaceful. I wanted to enjoy my life, to be able to relax and to be with people harmoniously. This was impossible given my stress levels and incessant thinking. I attended various courses and tried to 'program' my mind to make it quieter. That approach failed, so I booked a few sessions with a life coach. Thankfully she introduced me to meditation.

I recall visiting her one day for a session. I arrived there a few minutes early and was sitting in my car on the road outside of her house. It was a still and cloudy day and there was nobody around. I took the opportunity to meditate with my eyes open and I experienced something completely new. It was like there was something else that I couldn't see, hear, taste, smell or touch. In parallel, I was aware of the road, cars, houses, trees, and the normal stuff you'd observe on a housing estate. The experience was intriguing and impossible to explain. It was like there was some other dimension or realm. I was completely sober at the time. I recall my mind being unusually and perfectly silent. The experience only lasted a few seconds; then I returned to my state of incessant thinking. On reflection, I believe my ego was scared by the experience. It wasn't prepared to sit and go into whatever I connected with.

Years later, after learning more about meditation and spiritual teachings, I realized what I'd experienced was common for many beginners at the start of their meditation journey. It was a temporary and very intense, higher state of consciousness.

I carried on with the meditation practice. Later connected with Eckhart Tolle's teachings. I read his book *The Power of Now*[1] three times and only understood a small amount of it at an intellectual level. There was something that kept drawing me back in to read it. I then started watching his videos and slowly gained more of an understanding of his teachings. Many years later I connected with Buddhism. I traveled to different parts of the world attending retreats at monasteries and spent time speaking with different teachers including Buddhist monks. I then became involved with a Buddhist movement in the United Kingdom. I attended many group retreats, solitary retreats, experienced spiritual friendship and studied a range of Buddhist teachings. This was particularly helpful. For the first time I was introduced to a set of guidelines to help me with personal ethics. I began practicing basic principles including being mindful, kind and truthful. I was surprised at how powerful these guidelines were and how they cultivated a more peaceful mind. Life was becoming harmonious. Later, I started teaching others meditation and entered into an ordination training process with a view to joining the movement.

After some time, I reached a point where I knew that I needed spiritual independence. I wanted freedom to explore other spiritual teachings in depth and spend time with teachers outside of the movement, so I let go of my connections there. Spiritually speaking I entered into a blank space. After a short time, I returned to Eckhart Tolle's teachings and was able to understand them more. Years later, I went on to study and teach Yoga philosophy.

I've been practicing meditation and mindfulness for many years, studying with a range of teachers from different religions. During this time, I've trained and coached hundreds of people in these areas. I've also helped people to find and deepen their spiritual dimension, with a focus on applying spiritual teachings in everyday life. My first book, *Being Present*[2], was published in 2018, around the time of writing this book. *Being Present* is a synthesis of spiritual teachings and personal insights that can be applied to help you cultivate a peaceful mind, live skillfully, and experience a spiritual connection through the power of the present moment. The teachings in *Being Present* point the way to gaining freedom from becoming lost in unhelpful thoughts and emotions.

Creating *Living a Life of Harmony*

Creating this book, *Living a Life of Harmony,* was spontaneous and straightforward. I wasn't consciously planning to write a second book. I use the word *consciously* here as my subconscious mind was creating the book long before I became aware of it. Once the broad structure of the book was completed, I was confident it would be of benefit to myself and others. What I appreciate about this book is its simplicity. A description of the way the universe unfolds, followed by seven guidelines that can be applied in any life situation, to cultivate a peaceful mind and live a life of harmony. After binging on religious and philosophical teachings for many years I needed to clarify my own spiritual understanding and have a list of guidelines to follow, that were simple and relevant. I practiced The Guidelines explained in this book for myself and discussed them at length with others. I very quickly realized they were evidently practical, they significantly reduced suffering and cultivated peace.

I reflected deeply on my own life situation – asking myself what causes peace and happiness; versus what causes stress and suffering. There was a direct correlation between my approach to life and the results I observed. When I followed The Guidelines, life flowed harmoniously. Things weren't always easy and pleasant, but psychologically I was at peace. When I did the opposite of what The Guidelines recommend, I would always create stress for myself and others. Like most people, I'd regularly talk to friends and acquaintances about their experiences in life – learning what they've been doing and how it affected them. I continuously noticed the same results. If people followed The Guidelines, they'd be at peace. If they did the opposite, they'd create stress. I also noticed that generally speaking, when people followed The Guidelines, they were happy. And those who did the opposite were unhappy – regardless of how they might project themselves. Once I'd acknowledged all of this it felt right to share what I'd discovered.

It's my hope that for you, this book will serve as a friend and reference guide, to help you live skillfully and peacefully. Become fully aligned with what is, what's happened and what's to come. Live a life of harmony within The Process. Let us begin…

POINTS FOR REFLECTION

1. When spiritual teachings align with science and logic, you've found the truth.

2. The Guidelines are:
   a. Honor the body.
   b. Be present, bringing awareness and acceptance into every moment.
   c. Act with kindness, considering everyone and everything.
   d. Understand the truth, communicating it selectively and skillfully.
   e. Do only what needs to be done.
   f. Harmoniously obtain and retain only what you need.
   g. Apply The Guidelines to your digital device usage.

3. These simple guidelines, enable far reaching benefits for those who understand and follow them.

4. The Guidelines are not there to help you achieve this or that. Paradoxically though, if you do apply them, you are more likely to set and achieve goals that are aligned with what's needed.

5. Following The Guidelines will mean changes for you. Possibly big changes.

6. For most, it takes time and effort to understand and apply The Guidelines consistently.

7. The Process created you. And now you, its creation, are becoming aware of the creator.

8. The Process is becoming more aware of itself through its own creation.

9. The Guidelines align beautifully with any quality religion or philosophy.

10. I use the words *aligned* and *misaligned* throughout the book. Unless stated otherwise, I'm referring to alignment and misalignment with The Guidelines and The Process.

11. I use the words *aligned* and *skillful* interchangeably. Also, I use the words *misaligned* and *unskillful* interchangeably.

Chapter One

The Process

What is The Process?

EVERYTHING IS CONNECTED to form The Process. You can prove this for yourself with some simple examples. I'm assuming you're dressed right now as you read this book. Look at the clothes you're wearing. How did they get there? Probably because you dressed yourself earlier in the day. Getting dressed was a process. Bring to mind a politician. How did he or she get elected? Again, through a process. Whether it was ethical or corrupt, it was still a process. A sequence of events that led to an outcome. Sometimes you can evidence a process directly, like with the clothes example. And sometimes you can infer it. For example, if there are puddles everywhere outside, then it's usually safe to assume it's been raining. That's inference. In some cases, like the politician example, for most of us, you can only imagine or assume what might have happened. Even if you can't prove or explain things in detail, there's always a smaller process involved in everything that's a part of The Process. The Process is the BIG process; the universal process I outlined in the introduction.

You can observe The Process at different levels. Switching on the kettle and boiling water is a straightforward example. You can observe The Process at more subtle levels. At the time of writing this book my daughter was studying Biochemistry. Biochemists look at biochemical processes within living organisms. They find processes that connect molecules. These are processes like with the kettle example, but at a far subtler level. Oxygen created by photosynthesis is another subtler process. People may investigate processes over long time periods like global warming and changes in sea levels. There are an infinite number of processes. The sequence of events you take to obtain a passport is a process. Your body follows a process from birth to death. The earth can be viewed as a process with its creation, existence and ultimate destruction. They are all processes. Everything that happens is part of many processes and also a part of The Process.

As you read through this book you'll notice that I use the word "process" frequently. When I refer to a process or processes with a small "p," I mean smaller processes that connect together and operate at different levels. When I refer to "The Process" I mean the overall universal process, that all the smaller processes are a part of. All smaller processes are connected together either directly or indirectly, to form The Process. The Process is universal and infinite. It has no beginning or end. It's connected to an infinite source that I'll refer to later.

Why is understanding The Process important?

Why is understanding The Process and keeping it in mind so important? There are a number of reasons. Believing untruths and misunderstanding The Process, always leads to harm. A tragic example of this was reported in the news. Although I cannot personally confirm the truth about what I'm going to share, it does serve as a graphic example of misunderstanding The Process and its consequences. People in a remote village were reported to believe that an endangered tiger was a shape-shifter. A shape-shifter is a being that changes its form. This is the kind of thing mentioned in folklore and fiction. The news story explained how the villagers killed the tiger with a spear and hung it up for display from the rafters of a public house.

Can you bring to mind any examples of harm caused, when people misunderstood the truth? Many of the world's religions and philosophies place great emphasis on valid knowledge and truth, to avoid suffering and spread kindness. Fortunately, the more you understand The Process and its accompanying guidelines, the more you'll understand the truth and act skillfully. The Yoga Sutras[3] point to this, providing a useful framework for confirming whether knowledge is valid.

You can use any of these three methods to prove something is truthful:

1. You directly evidence something through observing it yourself.
2. You make an inference, like in the puddles and rain example earlier.
3. You obtain the facts from a trusted source.

In the story provided earlier, if the villagers understood the truth about the tiger, they may not have killed it. I'll explain more about this when we discuss the guideline "Understand the truth, communicating it selectively and skillfully" in Chapter Six.

The more you understand The Process, the more you communicate truthfully. If you state an opinion rather than facts, you'll caveat what you say with something like "my opinion is." This was evident in the tiger story.

I didn't talk to the villagers to confirm their belief about shape-shifters, or see the tiger killed with my own eyes. I just read it in the news, so I cannot confirm that it actually happened. Only that the news reported it. I can truthfully state that there were beautiful flowers in my neighbor's garden today, because I evidenced them with my own eyes. Many people are lazy and inaccurate with their communication. They claim things are true, when they may be false. People appreciate you speaking the truth and working with facts. Opinions are different to facts. Opinions are fine and have their place, so long as they're communicated truthfully as opinions, rather than untruthfully as facts.

The Process is important because it universally creates, sustains and destroys everything. It represents all of nature and the interconnections between form at all levels. Form consists of thoughts, feelings, bodily sensations and things you are aware of though your senses. In addition, it consists of all the form-based stuff out there that you cannot directly sense, like oxygen or sounds that are outside your frequency of hearing. It's literally everything. The intelligence within The Process controls all form.

Your body consists of form and is part of The Process. Most people believe there's something fixed about them. Some kind of fixed identity. That's untrue. There's nothing fixed about any of us. We're all temporary and changing every moment. Every few years every cell in our bodies changes. We are minute processes within The Process. If there was a person in your city or town who created, sustained and destroyed everything, they'd be deemed important. What I'm discussing here is the overarching Process that includes everything. It spans the whole universe. It's ultimately important due to its infinite scale and power. It makes sense to understand The Process and to respect it.

Who owns The Process?

So far, we've been unable to scientifically prove who the owner of The Process is. There are plenty of theories and descriptions you'll find in philosophies and religions. Is it owned or does it own itself? How can something infinite be owned? If it is owned, who or what owns the owner?

A few people believe we're part of a computer simulation. It's an interesting hypothesis. And one which I don't rule out. A few years ago, we wouldn't have dreamed about how powerful computers are these days, with approximately nine trillion text messages being sent each year, over a billion videos viewed each day on mobile devices, and the increase in virtual reality technology. The statistics are staggering. I'm sure they'll be dwarfed shortly after this book has been published. The fact that something the size of one brain can deliver such a high definition virtual reality experience in the form of dreams whenever we sleep, shows that it would be possible for us to be part of a computer simulation. Much of the time when we're dreaming, the simulation, if indeed it is a simulation, appears to be so real that we don't even know we're dreaming! A dream is like a computer simulation, with the computer being our mind. How do we know there isn't a larger computer than controls all the smaller computers?

If we are part of a computer simulation, then who owns the simulation? Are they part of some wider simulation? Any computer simulation like this would have to be part of a bigger simulation or process, which leads us back to The Process. If you do believe we're part of a simulation that's OK and you'll still benefit from what I'm going to share with you. The Guidelines then become the rules for living a life of harmony within the simulation.

I don't know if anybody owns The Process. What I do know is that The Process exists because it can be clearly evidenced. For the sake of what's to follow in this book, we don't need to be concerned about the owner of The Process. That said, I would like to share an assumption about The Process with you. I'm assuming that the owner, if there is an owner, doesn't change The Guidelines. Once you learn more about The Guidelines and explore them for yourself, you'll realize they're eternal. As eternal as our minds can imagine, based upon the information that we have to hand about history, and what we might predict for the future. This is one of those areas where I'd like you to either trust my judgement or at least be prepared to work with the assumption for now.

Is The Process orderly?

The Process is orderly as it aligns with The Guidelines. The Process rewards people and all sentient beings, that follow The Guidelines, and corrects those who do not. Strictly speaking, it's not consciously rewarding or correcting. That's just how it feels to us. The truth is that it's simply evolving. The Process learns from its own creative mistakes as we see them. Let's take an example. If a human being understands the truth about something and communicates it selectively and skillfully, they'll be rewarded with greater peace of mind. They may also be rewarded with other things like more harmonious relationships and greater influence.

In many countries, if a dog viciously attacks a human, it will be destroyed. If we fail to care for our bodies, we become ill. There are billions of examples of situations where you can link actual experiences with The Guidelines. Many religions believe that rewards or corrections span multiple lifetimes. This means you may enjoy rewards in this life that were earned through following The Guidelines in previous lives. We often hear stories about people who have been harmful and appear to get away with suffering the consequences. They die without receiving the corrections. The energy associated with such deeds is always refined at some point. It's part of evolution and The Process will often respond to such things later in time. Maybe in a future life.

Fortunately, there is a way of proactively avoiding corrections, other than by learning through your mistakes. It's by studying and practicing spiritual teachings. This is one of the main reasons why humans have installed countless religions over the centuries. Religions encourage followers to learn and practice spiritual teachings. When The Process observes you aligning with a particular guideline or even part of a guideline, it won't bother you with the associated corrections. In that respect, you'll be free from suffering and live more harmoniously. It's analogous to children following the rules set by their parents. They experience more peace, because they don't get corrected or punished.

I find it far more enjoyable to learn and practice The Guidelines rather than to suffer corrections. A moderate amount of fear and anxiety about The Process and its corrections, can be helpful. Many people reject fear and punishment when raised in a religious or spiritual context. Usually because teachings or teachers articulate the workings of such things in an inappropriate way. Corrections feel horrid to our egos and yes, the suffering is unpleasant. Corrections are natural though and needed for us to evolve. They provide learning moments. Once you understand that, you'll appreciate being fearful of corrections. You'll also positively frame any suffering you experience through the corrections you receive. Over time and as you evolve, fear and suffering reduce. Once they're gone altogether, you're awakened. You cease to be a manifestation of The Process altogether and you are purely its source.

You may be able to recall when you felt The Process was disorderly. I've known people whose children died at a young age through no apparent fault of their own. Why is this? How does that fit with The Process? These are difficult questions to answer, because we don't wish to accept things that we disagree with. Especially things that appear to go against our natural wishes. Many parents would be in complete resistance if their children died at a young age. They might claim the death was 'wrong.' At least for a while. They might say "My child was so kind and honest. They wouldn't harm a fly. This is so cruel. It isn't right. Why did this happen to them?" I can understand why people ask such questions. With the limited knowledge they have about The Process, the situation doesn't make any sense. In a similar way you might ask why over fifty million people were killed in the second world war, or why terrorist acts are committed.

All the tragic things that we experience and hear about in life needed to happen. In the world wars, the decisions made by those in leadership positions and the surrounding actions, led to the loss of millions of lives. Sometimes biological or geological conditions mean that people die well in advance of the average age of death. The Process causes this. The Process isn't bad. It's learning and evolving. It makes what we may perceive as 'mistakes' and causes what we perceive as 'harm,' just like we do. When it makes mistakes, they may be on a grand scale or seem very personal to us. It may be The Process makes our planet so hot and unpredictable that our species is completely wiped out. Most people will disagree with that. The Process creates, sustains and ultimately destroys everything. Destruction, in particular, is one of the hardest things for us to accept – due to the fact that our egos get attached to things. The Process regularly delivers outcomes that are completely at odds with our personal agendas. It's orderly in relation to The Process and disorderly in relation to our egos.

Who am I?

If The Process consists of everything, then who are you? Now I'm going to tell you something that you might find difficult to digest. *The unique combination of form that you may associate with who you are, only exists in the present moment.* Then what was there is gone. It's replaced with something new in the next moment. This is contrary to what most people believe – that there's something fixed about them, which they carry through life. There's not. Your mind and body are examples of small processes within The Process. What you see when you look in the mirror is a process. When you feel sensations in your body, this is a process. Emotions are a process. All the thoughts that pop into your mind are processes. Your mind and body can be viewed as a single process or a collection of processes.

We refer to ourselves, others, and things, using names. When we do that, we're conceptualizing and labeling temporary processes. That level of conceptual thinking and labeling is required to function in the world. As you do this, it's helpful to keep in mind that you, others, and everything else, is a temporary process. What you think about and refer to, are mind generated concepts and labels, not fixed entities.

When I tell people this, they sometimes react negatively, which is their ego reacting. There are many definitions of what our ego is. The ego I'm referring to here, is your false sense of self that identifies and attaches to many of the changing things contained within The Process. The deluded ego believes that collectively, these things represent some kind of fixed form-based existence.

Religions and philosophies have different views on who a person really is in their formless essence. This will never be proved scientifically because science is form-based. For the same reason, who a person really is, cannot be articulated in a book like this. Personally, I *know* that who I am transcends form. I can describe who I am as the intelligence within The Process. I would like to reassure you that the teachings in this book are highly beneficial, regardless of who you think you might be. I will also point now that as you read the book, your view of who you think you might be might change.

Am I dreaming this?

It's impossible to prove whether you and everything you experience really exists. As I mentioned earlier, you may think it does, when actually you might be part of some simulation or experiment. Are you in a dream? Dreams can feel as real as so-called 'real life.' You can't prove you're not in a simulation or dream right now. You can prove you're in a process though. If most people reflect on their dreams, they soon realize they had no idea they were in a dream at the time. It felt real. All dreams are also part of The Process. The 'life' you think you have now may be part of a dream.

Over time, you'll be able to apply The Guidelines as well in your dreams as you can in 'real life.' It helps to aim for this, because your dreams are part of The Process. The form that your mind creates and your behaviors within dreams leave mental impressions, and inform your future interactions with The Process. It's all part of the law of karma. Every action, even something as subtle as a thought within a dream, has a consequence. It's logical when you consider The Process. And I know this to be true because I've experienced it for myself – I've had thoughts and feelings towards people in my dreams, which have impacted how I think and feel about them when I'm awake.

Obvious and subtle processes

Earlier in this chapter, I introduced the concept of different levels of process. For example, the kettle boiling water may be viewed as an obvious process, which we can evidence easily. A subtler process might be the production of oxygen from photosynthesis. The process of photosynthesis keeps us alive, whilst being invisible to the naked eye. There's a hierarchy of control between these different levels of process. The subtle processes control the obvious processes. For example, photosynthesis makes it possible for a human being to live and boil a kettle, whereas you don't need to boil a kettle to enable photosynthesis.

Sometimes we believe that the obvious processes control the subtle processes – especially through human intervention. We believe that we create all sorts of wonderful vaccines and medicines. We're perceiving ourselves to be doing this at a conceptual level that our minds can compute. Whilst what's really happening, is that the subtler processes down at an atomic level, are driving and creating everything, including what we believe we're creating! I haven't really created this book, although I may claim that I have at a conceptual level. The subtler processes creating my impermanent existence are influencing things. They're more responsible for the book creation than I am. I find this whole area fascinating. Humans are conceptually constrained by how well their minds can observe processes. Even the world's best microscopes will only take you so far. My belief is that there's no end to how subtle the processes go. The subtlety or depth of The Process is infinite. This implies that if there is an owner of The Process, that owner must also be of an infinite nature. Only something infinite can own something infinite. The real truth, as I know it, is that the owner and the infinite creation that it manifests are all one.

Reflecting on The Process

By doing this we return to the present moment and become mindful. To be mindful means to be aware and accepting of bodily sensations, objects entering the senses, thoughts and feelings. From a place of presence or mindfulness, we act wisely following The Guidelines. All of this links together. You can reflect on The Process at any time.

 ” It's helpful to keep The Process in mind whenever we can.

There are many techniques you can use to enable this. I'll introduce a few of them to you here:

1 **Observe an object and consider the process that created it**

   For example, you can look at your phone and think about how it might have been envisioned, designed and produced. Then, how it's shipped to you. If there are any little scratches or marks on it, you can reflect on how they got there. Get the idea? Can you see how much history sits behind something as simple as a phone? You can go on and on with this exercise going further and further back in time. Only a minute or two is required to reflect on The Process, although you can do more, if you find it enjoyable. Thinking in this way can help you appreciate things and practice gratitude. In the previous example, real gratitude is not to the phone, people or events that led to it being in your possession. It's actually gratitude towards The Process. This is why gratitude feels so good. The Process rewards you for appreciating it.

2 **View the process within a moving or changeable object**

   The Ocean is a great example of this. When you observe or even imagine an Ocean, you can examine the waves and how they are all connected together. You notice the sparkling light on the waves is caused by the reflection from the sun. Through observing all of this, helps you reflect on The Process. Observing a person walk or the branches of a tree swaying, are other examples of this practice.

3 **Become aware of what's causing thoughts and feelings**

   Become aware of a thought or feeling. Then see if you can work out what caused it. Was it another thought or feeling? Something entering the senses? Simple examples include being aware of when you're feeling tired or excited. What caused that? You recall the face of an old friend. Why did that happen? This can be done spontaneously, whilst reflecting, or within a formal meditation sitting.

4 **Recite a phrase that reminds you of The Process**

   Examples here might be, "I know that I'm part of a bigger process," or "Everything happens for a reason."

5   **Examine your breath as a process**

This is one of my favorite ways of reflecting on The Process.
You simply bring awareness to your breath and watch all of its
constituent parts. Where it starts, finishes, its texture, speed, depth,
impact on the body and so on. You can do this spontaneously or
as part of a meditation practice. People have meditated on the
breath for thousands of years. This form of meditation enhances
concentration and cultivates a peaceful mind.

6   **Reflect on the different levels of process**

Look at a plant in your home. It may have ended up there through
an obvious process. Maybe you purchased it from a store and
brought it home. Now reflect on the subtler processes associated
with the plant. You can reflect on how it's using the energy of
sunlight to drive a process to produce its own food. Another
example of this is reflecting on how the energy from a battery slowly
reduces within an electrical device.

7   **Meditate on how you're connected**

To begin with, follow a basic meditation technique for a few
minutes. Concentration on the breath is a good option for
most people. Once your mind settles, continue meditating, but
contemplate how you're connected to the universe. Investigate the
air coming into and out of your body; that you're dependent upon
to live. Recognize the impact that the external temperature is having
on your body. Appreciate that memories stored in your mind are
due to past events that involved things and people external to you.
Consider how you've been affected by other people and situations.
Also, how you affect other people or situations. Acknowledge that
you're not truly independent or fixed, but part of a process.

The final reflection technique is powerful. If you can ask yourself questions
like these when you're alert and relaxed, you'll be amazed at what happens.
Most people understand that they're affected by external conditions. And
that their actions affect external conditions. It's obvious. We aren't truly
independent or unchangeable. However, most people spend a lot of their
time viewing themselves as separate. It's a form of delusion.

> 99 **Contemplating the truth that you're part of a process during meditation will deepen your 'knowing' of that truth.**

I can vividly remember the first time this happened for me during meditation. It was scary for my ego. And at the same time, I thought "Wow! I really am just part of something bigger." It was a deep and profound experience for me.

People experience this deepening of the truth in different situations. Nature provides opportunities. Also, when something significant happens in life where you're shocked at how little control you actually have over things. It's easy to forget this when you're coasting along in your bubble and your ego's agenda is being met. I'm sure The Process sometimes creates these shocks to wake people up and remind them of its nature – especially if their lifestyle or mindset has been relatively fixed for a period of time; or when they feel complacent or invincible.

How does The Process relate to being present?

In my first book *Being Present*, I highlight the wisdom that can be accessed from the present moment; and how you can create a structured practice to cultivate a peaceful mind. The second guideline in *Living a Life of Harmony* is dedicated to being present: "Be present, bringing awareness and acceptance into every moment." If this single guideline was followed consistently, that would be sufficient to fully align you with the needs of The Process. This is why so much emphasis was placed upon being present within my first book. What's more interesting is that this applies to any of The Guidelines. Progress in one guideline leads to progress in others. Similarly, regression in one guideline, causes a chain reaction of regression in others. The Guidelines are linked together in the same way as all other processes.

Within the book *Being Present*, I reference Presence many times using a capital 'P.' I'm implying here that there's something unconditioned and available to us that's a source of power, love and intelligence. This source is accessible through the present moment, but it can't be observed. We can't scientifically prove that Presence exists, due to its formless nature. It also can't be explained. You can't prove or explain something that's formless through form, including words, analysis or scientific experiment. Presence is something that certain people know is there. And it's reflected in the form that it creates. You don't need to believe in Presence, God, or anything like that to understand The Process. That said, by understanding The Process, your *knowing* of what's formless may come to pass.

How does The Process relate to God?

People either believe in God, don't believe in God, or keep an open mind. They might use titles including Allah and Brahman. The guidance I offer in this book can be used regardless of your beliefs in this area. Those who believe in God may view The Process as its manifestation. Or that God is The Process. God may also be viewed as being the space that holds The Process or even the owner of The Process. Those who do not believe in God may simply observe The Process for what it is, to the level that they can understand intellectually, working purely with the facts and evidence of the teachings.

As the author of this book, it feels right to share my position on this. Through the study of spiritual teachings and my own experience, I do sense an all-encompassing presence that appears to be within and outside of the form that's created by The Process. It's present everywhere I go and whatever I'm doing. I also use words like peace, stillness, emptiness and love to describe it. I believe that who I am is infinitely vaster than my limited mind and body. During the times when I'm connected with who I know I am, rather than my ego, it's a beautiful experience. This presence is the owner of The Process and it can be found within all of its form-based manifestations. I cannot prove or explain this any further. I know it to be true.

Spirituality & science

Over the years, spirituality and science have drawn closer together. Science is based on form or nature; understanding physical form through observation, experiment and analysis. Spirituality is involved with form and also the formless. By the formless, I mean the space between form. If you were able to look within an atom, you'd find empty space between the electrons and nucleus. Now it may be that there's stuff within that empty space that we're not able to observe. Some people call this 'dark matter.' Even if it were proven that there was subtler form within this space, then there would be space between or around that subtler form. Then we would be asking what that space consists of! There's no provable end to the investigation. It would be infinite, and this infinite nature represents spirit or spirituality. I interpret Juan Mascaró's translation of the Upanishads[4] pointing to this, when he refers to spirit as being incredibly minute and also incredibly vast.

Spirituality is about establishing a connection with the formless. This is why many spiritual practitioners meditate on subtle form, in order to move them towards a connection with the formless. An example of this is to start meditation with concentration on the breath. The breath is a form-based process. You can then refine your meditation by concentrating on something subtler like your own awareness, and then go deeper into that. Spiritual practice uses form in this way to move closer to and ultimately connect with, the formless.

When scientists observe and analyze form at a subtler level they are moving closer to a connection with spirit. In his commentary on the Yoga Sutras, Satchidananda[3] referred to scientists who explored deep into the atom, as yogis.

Another way in which science and spirituality have drawn closer together is through the increasing use of digital technology and the Internet. This is now widely used for the publishing of spiritual teachings and the hosting of online spiritual communities. People enjoy the freedom of being able to connect with others and practice from the comfort of their own home or another remote location. This removes the constraints associated with having a geographically local group to connect with. Real human contact is wonderful and needed. However, for many people in remote locations, multiple locations, or without the means to travel, the Internet is enabling them to spiritually connect and practice. This method is liberating for people who find it difficult or impossible to leave the home; like the sick, the elderly or those caring for others.

The Process is enabling this shift. It uses a variety of means to help what it creates understand itself, in addition to the common spiritual practices that might come to mind like study, meditation or prayer. Progression in science and technology is all part of The Process. For now, and I would guess that for the foreseeable future, this phenomenon will continue. And at some time, as with all things, it will pass.

Am I making my own choices?

If everything's a process, then you may be asking yourself whether you have any real choices in life. Every choice you make is informed by:

1 **Knowledge you've accumulated from your past conditioning**

   For example, you may have learned not to put your hand in a fire through getting burnt previously.

2   **Psychological skills you've developed**

You may have learned how to determine what tasks to complete during the day, through the skill of prioritizing. Another example is the ability to gauge how somebody may be feeling based on their appearance or behaviors. These are both psychological skills.

3   **Accessing the infinite intelligence from The Process**

This is the creative source for true choices. This is your opportunity to go beyond conditioned knowledge and psychological skills. The choices you make using this intelligence come from an unconditioned source. These choices are spiritually perfect.

What's interesting about this theory is that it contains a paradox. When you're accessing the infinite intelligence, you're not dependent upon past conditioning. However, conditions and time are required to allow you to evolve so that you can access the infinite intelligence more frequently. This is why people have followed spiritual practices for thousands of years. Spiritual practice, which includes you reading this book right now, is a manifestation of conditions in time, helping you access the unconditioned and timeless. In the same, way I cannot explain what the infinite intelligence is with words, but my words may guide you towards knowing it.

You can't really make your own choices because you don't exist. As I mentioned earlier, you are actually part of The Process. There's nothing fixed about you. It's fine to think about yourself as existing in order to function conceptually, so long as you also keep in mind that your existence is only a mental concept; an image or story that the mind has created. If you can view things in this way, you'll be liberated. Whilst also knowing that there is no self to liberate!

I believe this is one of the most challenging concepts to grasp and practice as a human being on the spiritual path. To act responsibly and align with The Process, you do need to take responsibility for yourself and meet your genuine obligations. Doing your best to follow The Guidelines, living harmoniously, and cultivating peace and kindness. And whilst you're doing all of that, you know at a deeper level that you aren't actually separate or ultimately responsible for the direction you take – what you truly are is a changing part of The Process directed by its intelligence.

POINTS FOR REFLECTION

1. An infinite number of connected processes at different levels span the whole universe. They are components within an overarching process called The Process.

2. Everything that happens is part of many processes and also part of The Process.

3. The Process has no beginning or end. It's connected to an infinite source.

4. The Process is important because it universally creates, sustains and destroys everything.

5. The intelligence within The Process controls all form.

6. There's nothing fixed about any of us. We're all temporary and changing every moment.

7. The unique combination of form that you may associate with who you are, only exists in the present moment.

8. Most people spend a lot of their time viewing themselves as separate. It's a form of delusion.

9. The Process is orderly as it aligns with The Guidelines.

10. Corrections are natural and needed for us to evolve. They provide learning moments.

11. Over time, as you evolve, fear and suffering reduce. Once they're gone altogether, you're awakened. You cease to be a manifestation of The Process altogether and return to its source.

12. The Process is not bad. It's learning and evolving.

Chapter Two

The Guidelines

I'VE DEDICATED A CHAPTER to each of the seven guidelines from Chapter Three. Each guideline chapter provides a thorough explanation, real life examples of its application, and specific practices. The final chapter talks through how to structure your general practice across all guidelines. What I'd like to offer you first, is some context. How The Guidelines originated and why they're necessary. I'll explain what differentiates The Guidelines from other lists offering spiritual guidance, and just as importantly, what aligns The Guidelines with those lists. It will help you understand how The Guidelines were created and their close connection to religions and spiritual philosophies. This understanding cultivates faith, motivation and confidence, in your practice.

How The Guidelines were created

I've studied and practiced spiritual teachings with help from many teachers and religions. I've spent time within religious movements, integrated with spiritual communities, attended many retreats and read a vast number of spiritual books. The key sources of my knowledge are Buddhism, Eckhart Tolle's teachings, yoga philosophy and my own insights. I've retained my spiritual independence rather than aligning with an individual philosophy or religion. This is common these days, with teachings accessible to the masses through the Internet and books. It's also common for people to informally synthesize teachings from different sources, adding their own insights to create a unique practice. This has been my path, for which I'm grateful.

Religions will generally communicate a lot of truth, along with some teachings that are distorted. The distortion may simply be a matter of articulation and interpretation. Sometimes, religious teachings are communicated in a way that doesn't lend itself to being understood correctly in a given time and context. This leads to misunderstanding. Spiritual teachings are only effective when they're communicated in a way that can be understood by followers. Teachings can also be corrupted due to egoic agendas operating at both individual and organizational levels. In either of these cases, the result is harmful to the those impacted, as it leads to a deluded way of thinking and behaving. A spiritual aspirant must always maintain a level of awareness and independent thinking, protecting themselves from distortion of the truth.

Truthful communication from each religion aligns perfectly with truthful communication from other religions. In this respect, all paths lead to the same destination. Examples of this are to cause no harm and to be truthful. Such guidance appears in many religions and works in practice, so it must be truthful and aligned with The Process. The idea of a single set of truths that religions are aligned with is not new. It's an area that has been explored for hundreds of years through perennial philosophy.

The first time I came across anything like The Guidelines was when I was studying Buddhist teachings. The five Buddhist precepts from the Theravada tradition are used as training principles to guide ethical behavior. My opinion of Eckhart Tolle's teachings, is that they bring their followers back to one central guideline, which is being in the present moment. Then we have the eight limbs of yoga providing practical advice on moral conduct and stages to reach enlightenment. Christianity offers The Ten Commandments. And there are Verses of the Ten Commandments in The Quran. Similar lists may be found in other religions and philosophies.

The Guidelines were created spontaneously, based upon what I'd experienced from other teachings, my own insights and life experience. They were not the result of some big study or analysis involving thousands of people. Once I'd typed them out, I looked at them curiously, as I'd not seen them before. What I found, which was no surprise, is they have many commonalities with existing and respected lists. Advice like not causing harm, truthfulness and non-greed have been offered for years.

What's different about The Guidelines is the clear prioritization on honoring the body and being present. These are at the top of the list for good reason, as the other guidelines are followed automatically when these two are mastered. Another distinction is the focus on only doing what needs to be done. In an increasingly busy society we need this guideline to help us prioritize, filter information, filter opportunities, focus on what's important and create space in our lives. The explicitness of "Harmoniously obtain and retain only what you need," counters the increasing problem we face with consumerism. The final distinction is an emphasis on applying all guidelines to our digital device usage. The phenomenal increase in digital device usage, including mobile phones, tablets and computers, must be catered for and at the heart of any modern framework of spiritual guidance. The Guidelines contain the truth and power of existing lists whilst allowing for today's challenges, enabling a fresh and evolutionary approach to spiritual practice.

To be honest with you, I don't know whether The Guidelines will be adopted widely. What I do know is that if The Guidelines were followed diligently by everybody, the world would be a more peaceful, harmonious, kinder and sustainable place. Following The Guidelines enables us to live a life of harmony.

The Guidelines

The seven guidelines are presented in the table below, stated positively and negatively. When you read The Guidelines in this format for the first time, it may be obvious that you prefer the positive or negative style. The positive and negative styles are included to allow for individual preferences and also to act as a teaching aid. Motivation works in two ways. You can be motivated towards doing something (guidelines stated positively) or away from doing something (guidelines stated negatively). These guidelines tap into both sides of motivation to encourage you to follow them.

Guideline stated positively	Guideline stated negatively
Honor the body	Do not harm the body
Be present, bringing awareness and acceptance into every moment	Do not become lost in thought
Act with kindness, considering everyone and everything	Do not be intentionally harmful or single-minded in your actions
Understand the truth, communicating it selectively and skillfully	Avoid excessive, harmful and false communication
Do only what needs to be done	Do not do what is unnecessary
Harmoniously obtain and retain only what you need	Do not obtain or retain more than you need
Apply The Guidelines to your digital device usage	Do not disregard The Guidelines in your digital device usage

The Guidelines

There is much to learn about The Guidelines, which is why each of them has its own dedicated chapter. The guideline text stated above simply explains *what* needs to be done. The next few chapters help you understand *how* to do it, taking your own personal situation into account.

,, Write The Guidelines down in a place where you can access them regularly and recite them on a daily basis.

This has been common practice in religions for centuries. I stored them in a note on my phone, read them daily and memorized them. I also recite them at the end of each meditation session. Talking about The Guidelines with others is another great way of memorizing them and exploring their benefits. If you memorize The Guidelines, you're more likely to recall them dynamically, when they're needed in daily life. Your subconscious mind can be trained to use The Guidelines to make decisions without needing to consciously think through everything. Through deep integration of The Guidelines, actions within your dreams will also become aligned, which is an important part of practice.

There are two options you have for using the rest of this book. You can read each guideline chapter in sequence to gain a deeper insight. Alternatively, you can head straight to the chapter that explains the guideline you'd like to start work on right away, and then return to the other guidelines later. Ideally, read The Guidelines chapters in the sequence they're presented. They're all connected; referencing each other. Each guideline will be summarized to provide a scene setter for the detail in the subsequent chapters.

,, Apply The Guidelines carefully, after understanding them well.

If The Guidelines were a product you could purchase at the mall, there would be a label on them saying "WARNING: Misapplication causes harm." The Guidelines need to be understood well. Read through the whole book carefully, allowing it to provide you with a good understanding of each guideline and their interconnectedness.

You can return to the book later and dip into individual chapters to refresh your knowledge. The book has been written in a way so that it can be reused time and time again. This allows you to read the same page on different occasions and learn more with each read.

The book is as much for reference as it is for the initial assimilation of The Process and guidelines. The content of the book is unchanged, whilst your situation and mindset are changeable. This is why you receive different teachings with every read.

> **Honor the body**
> STATED NEGATIVELY: Do not harm the body
> LOCATION: Chapter Three

This guideline is at the top of the list for good reason. Honoring your body is a form of kindness. In order to act with kindness, considering everyone and everything (another guideline) you start with your own body. Your body needs to be honored because it's the external manifestation of your part of The Process. By honoring the body, you're honoring The Process. Caring for the body supports the mind's functioning and helps you follow the other guidelines.

Chapter Three provides general advice on looking after the body covering the areas of diet, relaxation, sleep, physical activity, acceptance, energy and sexuality. Our bodies, by their nature, are unreliable. They become sick from time to time and naturally degrade as we reach old age. Some of us have parts of our bodies that we dislike. We may compare ourselves to others. It's for these reasons that accepting the body along with all of its imperfections, aches, pains, and more serious problems, is an essential part of honoring the body and supporting the mind. Managing energy and our approach to sexuality, are also important factors in applying this guideline.

> **Be present, bringing awareness and acceptance into every moment**
> STATED NEGATIVELY: Do not become lost in thought
> LOCATION: Chapter Four

This guideline can also be described as mindfulness or being present. The first two guidelines, one for the body and one for the mind, lay foundations for the rest. I define mindfulness as awareness and acceptance of bodily sensations, form coming in through the senses, feelings and thoughts, within the present moment. The opposite to this is being lost in thought about the past or future. It can be helpful to think about the past or future, so long as it happens consciously, without you losing awareness.

There's a direct correlation between this guideline and aligning your actions with The Process. You need awareness so that you can understand the present moment, internally and externally. Understanding and accepting the present moment, places you in the best possible position to take skillful action that's aligned with The Process. It's this alignment that provides you with peace of mind. Action may consist of thoughts, communication or physical action. Skillful action can also be complete stillness, silence, or a decision to take no action. The opposite is true here. Being lost in thought leads to unskillfulness, misalignment with The Process, harm and disharmony.

Being present or mindful is a big challenge for most of us. Honoring the body makes it much easier to practice. Making the effort to be present is a good investment, as this is a very special guideline. Mastery of this guideline leads to the automatic mastery of all other guidelines. Improvements in this guideline leads to improvements in others.

When you're present you tap into a source of wisdom that transcends you. It's the infinite intelligence within The Process. With its guidance you can achieve full and consistent alignment. When you're present, all of your actions are aligned with what The Process needs, with little conscious thought required. This is accompanied by a peaceful mind. The supportive relationships between this and the other guidelines are shown diagrammatically below. Being present has a special place at the center of The Guidelines.

Supportive Relationships between The Guidelines

> **Act with kindness, considering everyone and everything**
> STATED NEGATIVELY: Do not be intentionally harmful or single-minded
> in your actions
> LOCATION: Chapter Five

Within The Guidelines, kindness in relation to people, means being considerate, friendly and generous. The scope of kindness is wider than the person or people you're being kind to. It means that each action has kindness at its source and considers the whole, rather than just an individual or group. I'll give you a simple example. A father may have competing demands from his two young children. One of them is demanding food, whilst the other is crying as she's experienced a nasty bump on the head. An act of kindness here would be to prioritize caring for the child with the bump on the head. You can see this would be the right thing to do overall, whilst not appearing to be kind in the eyes of the hungry child.

We're looking for kindness that considers everybody and prioritizes wisely, rather than direct kindness towards everybody. Direct kindness towards everybody is impossible. Even if we knew the actions we should take to be directly kind to everybody, we wouldn't have enough time or energy to complete the task. We apply kindness in the opportunities presented to us by The Process and do our best to consider the whole, as well as specific individuals or groups.

The scope of kindness is wider than just considering people. It includes all animals, insects, plants, objects and everything here on earth and beyond. It includes simple actions like how we close a cupboard door or drive our cars. We do so kindly. This means shutting cupboard doors carefully. And driving our cars in a way that's kind to the car, other drivers, passengers, pedestrians, and nature. Practicing kindness with simple everyday actions empowers us to approach our more substantial and complex actions kindly.

> **Understand the truth, communicating it selectively and skillfully**
> STATED NEGATIVELY: Avoid excessive, harmful and false communication
> LOCATION: Chapter Six

This guideline encourages us to take responsibility for understanding the truth and communicating it skillfully. Skillful communication means we consciously select what we communicate and how we communicate, rather than unconsciously saying or writing whatever pops into our heads without any kind of filter applied. Skillful communication is rooted in kindness – it dovetails with the previous guideline. This is why the guideline on kindness is listed before the guideline on communication. Kindness is a foundation for skillful communication. Skillful communication is aligned with what The Process needs to evolve.

This guideline emphasizes communicating selectively. For many people, this means communicating less. When we communicate excessively it has less impact and makes it harder for those we are communicating with to process the information. As we evolve, we become more comfortable with silence and listening – communicating with skill and impact.

> Communicating selectively means that we consciously consider what we should be communicating to whom, allowing kindness to guide us.

Do only what needs to be done
STATED NEGATIVELY: Do not do what is unnecessary
LOCATION: Chapter Seven

There are always more things to do than we have time for. We can fill our lives with so much activity, that it's impossible for us to act mindfully and in alignment with The Guidelines. When we're too busy and lost in thought, we lower the quality of our interactions with people and the things we create. This is because we're working on auto-pilot rather than being present. When we're truly in the present moment, we do what's required of us by The Process. Whilst being present, activities are completed with a peaceful mind and often accompanied by enjoyment or enthusiasm.

> We need to take time for our bodies and minds to relax. For most of us, this means doing less – doing only what needs to be done.

On the whole, most of us do far more than we really need to. I believe this is linked to the economy, and political power. Consumerism is also a factor. An increase in the number of things people purchase places demands on the amount of money they need to maintain their lifestyle; and often the amount of time they spend working to earn that money. Things are replaced in the name of style and fashion, long before they've reached the end of their practical useful life. This cultural issue puts an inordinate amount of pressure on individuals to work harder, creating enough income to pay for their luxuries. It also means that people have to spend more time shopping for things, installing them, returning them if they're faulty or unsuitable, and disposing of things that are deemed surplus to requirements.

This guideline is about consciously selecting what we spend our time doing. We move towards only doing what The Process needs and dropping unnecessary activities. Interestingly, when we do this, all of our personal needs get met, including opportunities to enjoy pleasure and achieve goals.

> **Harmoniously obtain and retain only what you need**
> STATED NEGATIVELY: Do not obtain or retain more than you need
> LOCATION: Chapter Eight

This guideline covers obtaining and retaining items. Examples of items are homes, cars, clothes, gadgets, books, make-up, crockery etc. Items also include subtler digital things we own like files on our computer or desktop icons. You obtain only what you need, and what you don't need, you release. If the unnecessary item's an object, you may sell it, give it away or dispose of it. This simplifies life and creates space. Simplicity leads to less activity, which supports the previous guideline. Spaciousness helps us to practice awareness and acceptance.

You may have noticed the word 'harmoniously' used within this guideline title. Obtaining things harmoniously means doing so in accordance with The Guidelines, ensuring qualities like awareness, kindness and truthfulness are present in our actions to acquire what we need. We observe another example here, where consumerism adds to the challenge of following The Guidelines.

> **Apply The Guidelines to your digital device usage**
> STATED NEGATIVELY: Do not disregard The Guidelines in your digital
>   device usage
> LOCATION: Chapter Nine

Given the existential use in digital devices it's right to have a guideline that supports their usage. Digital devices include things like phones, tablets, computers and TVs. At the time of writing, I read statistics claiming that many people are spending around half of each day staring at screens. There are things we can do to reduce this. However, given the way things are shaping up culturally, the bulk of us must accept that a substantial percentage of our life will be spent in this way. Using digital devices is no different from any other activity as far as The Process is concerned.

> **Applying The Guidelines to digital device usage is just as important as applying them at times when we're not using digital devices.**

When we're using digital devices, we need to be applying the first six guidelines. For example, we need to care for the body by ensuring that our posture is suitable if we're using a computer. When we're watching TV, we need to stay present and aware, rather than getting lost in our thoughts about the content or other things. When messaging people, we need to communicate the truth selectively and skillfully. We should only use our devices when there's a real need. Hopefully you get the idea. We'll go into more detail on this in Chapter Nine.

Progress rather than perfection

I must confess that I have much work to do, before I can claim that I follow The Guidelines perfectly. I'm work in progress and don't view myself as being enlightened. I'm sure there are many people out there who are far more spiritually evolved than I am. I don't see myself as highly advanced in that way. What I can say though, is that in my years of practicing, the bulk of which have been independent of organizations or religions, I've made great progress. Considering the difficult conditions earlier in life and how frantic my mind was, I've come a long way in a relatively short space of time. This is primarily as a result of diligently applying spiritual teachings and observing my own mind. The Process has organized things so that my path has been to learn and apply what I'm presenting to you. This is what qualifies and enables me to write spiritual books and teach in the way that I do.

When I follow The Guidelines, I'm peaceful. When I disregard them, I suffer. The Guidelines are there to point you in the right direction. They're a vision and it's right to be working towards them, rather than expecting yourself to be perfect. The truth is, you are perfect just as you are at this moment in time because the Process has made you that way. Applying The Guidelines is a practice. Delight in any progress you make. Occasionally, people report sudden spiritual awakenings. If they're truly awakened they'll follow The Guidelines perfectly from that point onwards for the rest of their life, whilst they're psychologically well. For most of us, we awaken gradually. To accelerate towards awakening, we work to understand The Process and intensify our practice of The Guidelines.

Paradoxically, when you disregard the guidelines and do the opposite, you often subsequently get an opportunity to apply them. The Process is generous in that way. Let me give you an example. Assume that in a moment of tiredness when you're lost in thought, you speak to a friend in a way that's unkind. It causes the friend stress and you experience feelings of guilt. Three guidelines have been disregarded here: (i) be present, bringing awareness and acceptance into every moment (ii) act with kindness, considering everyone and everything and (iii) understand the truth, communicating it selectively and skillfully. Maybe, ahead of the unskillfulness you disregarded the guideline relating to caring for the body, causing you to become tired. Can you see how disregarding The Guidelines links together and creates a chain reaction? Often, disregarding one guideline leads to you disregarding others. In this situation, subsequently, you have opportunities to apply the guidelines that you disregarded. For example, you may respond by becoming present, sensitively apologizing to your friend, making a kind gesture, and ensuring that you have more rest to help keep yourself alert.

Decision making & conflicts

We have situations from time to time when we're faced with a complex decision. We think through the pros and cons, seek advice, consider our experience, tune into our intuition and then still feel baffled about what to do! These are golden opportunities to use The Guidelines. Simply scan through the table found earlier in this chapter and then allow your mind to ponder on the decision. Often an answer will come quickly. If it doesn't, then you can ask your subconscious to process it in the background. Then, at some point, the right answer will pop into your conscious mind and it will be aligned with The Process. The more you understand and apply The Guidelines, the higher the probability of the right decision being made.

Teaching and groups

This book explains how to apply The Guidelines within your life situation. It's a spiritual self-help guide. There are other ways the content can be used. Firstly, as a teaching aid. If you're a spiritual teacher already, you can use what's in this book to help your students. If you're not a spiritual teacher, don't try to become one. Instead, practice The Guidelines diligently, taking opportunities to teach, as and when they're presented to you. Becoming a spiritual teacher isn't something you can learn by taking a course and gaining qualifications. You should never force spiritual teachings onto people or even offer teachings unless they're requested. It's not like training to be a pilot or doctor. The Process informs you when the time is right for you to offer spiritual teachings, which may be in this lifetime, future lifetimes or not at all.

The Guidelines may be applied to groups as well as individuals. It can be a group of any size. It may be a family, community, commercial organization, country or even a planet. Broadly speaking, the greater the group is in alignment with The Guidelines, the more the group will exist harmoniously. A group can live a life of harmony. The flip side to this is when a group is misaligned with The Guidelines. Misalignment at a group level causes suffering for the group in the same way that it does for the individual. You can see this operating at all levels. For example, on the whole, families that collectively align with The Guidelines will be more peaceful and well regarded. Businesses that are misaligned with The Guidelines will tend to suffer losses or closure. Religions, communities, countries, friendship groups and all other groups, are impacted in the same way.

Those who have greater influence within groups will impactfully communicate positive and negative examples of alignment to other group members. This can ripple out and impact millions of people in some cases. The Process enjoys selecting certain people and making them more influential than others. Some people encourage peace and love. Others cause a great deal of harm. When individuals or groups suffer through being harmed by something or someone external to them, The Process is training them to become more aligned with how things need to be. They're receiving corrections. We can all learn through our suffering.

The Process & The Guidelines in action

You can reflect upon how alignment with The Guidelines helps people live peacefully within The Process. This helps build faith in applying The Guidelines and deepens your understanding of them. Start with yourself.

> **Take a little time out during the day to reflect on the things that lead to a peaceful mind, and the things that cause stress.**

Whatever action you take, be that thought, communication or physical action, when you're aligned with The Guidelines, your mind will be peaceful during the action. If you need to think, your thoughts will be peaceful. When you disregard The Guidelines, your mind will be destabilized and lost in thought during the action. This is a form of stress. Stress is caused by being misaligned with the present moment.

The feelings associated with any action will be pleasant, neutral or unpleasant. Alignment with The Guidelines produces pleasant or neutral feelings. Disregard of The Guidelines produces unpleasant feelings and suffering. This is the two sides of karma. The action taken and the results or fruits from the action. It's often difficult to say when the results will come to fruition. Many religions believe that karma spans lifetimes. This implies you can receive the results of actions from past lives in this life. It also implies that deeds in this life may have consequences in future lives. Personally, I choose to believe in multi-life karma. It aligns with The Process. Who we truly are is never born. And who we truly are doesn't die. Even although our bodies are created and destroyed. This is why the karma we create and experience spans lifetimes. Your body is being used by The Process as a vehicle for evolution. My biggest motivator for believing this, is that it helps me to accept personal events that I can't account for. Sometimes things happen to me and I can't work out why or trace them back to events in the past. In addition, believing in multi-life karma helps me stay aligned with The Guidelines on the basis that I wish to be free from suffering in this life and future lives.

We can observe karma unfolding in the lives of others and learn from them. This may be by directly observing people we are with, observing people we see in the media, or hearing about events from others. The way people interact with The Process and The Guidelines is fascinating. I find it both educational and interesting to observe.

> 〞 Contemplate how alignment with The Guidelines impacts others in their daily lives.

It's often wise to keep this as a private activity rather than something you communicate. This will prevent any untruthful judgements being projected. Things are too complex to consistently and accurately determine the causes and effects in people's lives. During the observation you can temporarily view the whole situation as being part of a game or simulation. It may or may not be. This will help you observe The Process. Also, keep in mind that the best person to observe is yourself. On the whole, you should keep your focus there. Your practice should always come back to you.

Keep in mind that it's impossible for me to cover absolutely every point and context area for The Guidelines. Instead, I've majored on what I see as being some of the key points and provided examples from my own life experience. You'll need to take responsibility for applying The Guidelines in your own way. Aligning yourself with The Guidelines allows you to access more wisdom; and more wisdom enables more alignment.

POINTS FOR REFLECTION

1. Progression in one guideline leads to progression in others. Similarly, regression in one guideline, can cause a chain reaction of regression in others.

2. Honoring the body and being present, are at the top of the list of guidelines for a good reason. The other guidelines are followed automatically when these two are mastered.

3. If The Guidelines are followed diligently by everybody, the world will be a more peaceful, harmonious, kinder and sustainable place.

4. If you memorize The Guidelines, you're more likely to recall them dynamically, when they're needed in your daily life.

5. To accelerate towards awakening, we work to understand The Process, and intensify our practice of The Guidelines.

6. Scan through The Guidelines to help yourself with complex decision making.

7. Apply The Guidelines carefully, after understanding them well.

8. We can all learn through our suffering.

9. Take a little time out during the day to reflect on events that lead to a peaceful mind, and events that cause suffering.

10. Spiritually speaking, the best person to observe is yourself. On the whole, you should keep your focus there. Your practice should always come back to you.

11. When awareness and acceptance of every moment is practiced, The Guidelines will always be followed.

12. Aligning yourself with The Guidelines allows you to access more wisdom; and more wisdom enables more alignment.

Chapter Three

Honor the Body

Stated negatively: Do not harm the body

IF YOU UNDERSTAND the Guidelines well, and follow them diligently, you'll live a life of harmony; enjoying a peaceful mind, where thinking takes place only when it's needed. The mind quietens through regular practice. A peaceful mind is the ultimate fruit. Unless you believe there's an enlightened state beyond this, in which case it's the penultimate fruit. Given this, you may be wondering why a guideline for the body has been placed at the top of the list. This is due to the substantial influence the body has over the mind. It's also at the top because many people don't prioritize honoring and caring for the body, which makes it difficult, if not impossible, to follow the other guidelines.

Guideline: Honor the Body

Yoga philosophy places a great deal of emphasis on honoring the body. Many people assume that yoga is merely a physical practice used for making the body strong and flexible. It's much more than that; containing a range of other practices including ethical standards, self-discipline, meditation, and spiritual observances, all culminating in awakening or enlightenment. Nowadays, Yoga is taught with emphasis on the body, whereas traditionally, it was much more about the mind. The justification for this might be that if the body is flexible and strong, the mind will follow. There's truth in that statement, which you can evidence for yourself. Recall times in your life when you've felt healthy, tired or sick. You'll notice a correlation between a healthy body and the mind's ability to remain peaceful and concentrated. The reverse is true. A tired or sick body makes it much harder for us to keep the mind functioning in the right way, and aligned with The Guidelines.

A healthy body *helps* the mind work effectively with The Guidelines. If the body is weak or sick, The Guidelines can still be followed, but it may prove more challenging. This is an important point, especially if your body is weak or sick.

> When you practice The Guidelines with a weak or sick body it's a great training – like lifting heavy weights to build muscle.

If you have an unwell body, it often means you have to apply more effort to keep the mind focused, so paradoxically this is giving the mind additional training and building its capacity to stay present. This guideline should be practiced regardless of whether you're sick or well. When you honor something, you respect it regardless of its condition. When you care for your body you are practicing the guideline relating to kindness. Whatever state your body is in, you can find ways to practice any of the guidelines. People can be peaceful and achieve wonderful things, despite having debilitating conditions. Achieving a peaceful mind is primary and of absolute importance. Achieving anything else is secondary and of relative importance.

Honoring the body

English Oxford Living Dictionaries[5] describe the verb 'honor' as regarding something with great respect and fulfilling an obligation. This applies to honoring the body. The body needs to be respected because it represents your part of The Process. By honoring the body, you are actually honoring

The Process. Through the very act of creating you, The Process is obliging you to respect your own body and mind.

Honoring the body can be broken down into these three components: Prioritization, non-harm and nourishment.

> **Prioritization means wherever possible, we place the genuine needs of the body first, above everything else.**

This reflects the guideline's priority within the list of guidelines. This can only be made possible after your life conditions have been properly adjusted. Like all guidelines, honoring the body takes time to master. The challenge when applying any of The Guidelines is that you've had periods in your life when you were not practicing them. During these times, you would have created all sorts of conditions, obligations and habits, that cannot be instantly undone or changed. For example, you may be in a job where the working hours means you have insufficient time to rest and relax. The Process doesn't expect you to quit your job instantly (although this may be the right thing to do in some cases), as that may end up causing more stress and harm overall. Instead, you set an intention to make whatever positive changes are required to your work situation, and then implement those changes in a way that's kind and skillful, which may take some time.

There are occasions from time-to-time where something else genuinely needs to take priority. For example, you may be driving on a highway and your body needs food. It wouldn't be right to just pull over to the side of the road where it's unsafe in order to eat a healthy meal! It would make sense to wait until you could find somewhere safe to eat. Another example is if your body needed sleep whilst you were walking home late at night through a busy town. It would be inappropriate to just lay down on the pavement and sleep there and then! It would make sense to wait until you returned home. Common sense is required when applying The Guidelines. Their application is never black and white. This is why being present is so important, as it allows us to use the wisdom within The Process to guide us, even in complex situations.

Back to the three components of honoring the body: Prioritization, non-harm and nourishment. The ideal or utopian situation with non-harm, is that we don't take any action that harms our body. Obvious examples of this include damaging our body through eating unhealthy foods, drugs misuse or forms of self-harming. At a subtler level this may include sitting in a posture that's painful, exercising to the point where it damages the body, exposing our skin to the hot sun for too long or not getting enough rest. Non-harm of the body is also understanding and managing the impact our thoughts and emotions have on the body. Aches and pains in the body are often due to emotional problems and may eventually lead to disease if left untreated. When we're aware enough to correlate bodily issues with emotional issues we can take informed action. For example, an intense relationship problem might be causing stress and resulting in headaches. Changing or letting go of that relationship may be an indirect way of honoring the body.

The final component is nourishing the body.

> Obvious guidance here is ensuring we're eating, sleeping, resting and exercising well.

Nourishing the body must be applied in conjunction with the guideline, "Do only what needs to be done." We can misread this guideline and think that it means spending an inordinate amount of time building muscles that we don't need for our day-to-day activities, overuse of cosmetic products, or doing things to create excessive amounts of sensuous pleasure. All of these things have their place in moderation where there's a genuine need. When we're consuming or doing something excessively, we're withdrawing more from the Process than is necessary and this always causes harm to ourselves and others. It's like going into overdraft with your bank account. It comes with a cost. And the more you go into your overdraft, the higher the charges. We'll explore the guideline, "Do only what needs to be done" in Chapter Six. There are many subtler ways we can nourish the body. Getting enough fresh air and considering the quality of air we expose ourselves to is an example of this. Managing our conditions to keep the body temperature regulated is another example. All of these things help keep the body peaceful, which in turn makes it easier to keep the mind peaceful and follow The Guidelines.

Diet

A balanced diet is essential for nourishing the body. This section will be kept brief on the basis that this area is well documented elsewhere. I will share a few pointers with you that have worked in my experience. Most importantly, keep your diet well balanced with food and drink containing carbohydrates, healthy fats, proteins, vitamins, minerals, fiber and water. I recommend you review the latest guidance on diet from trusted sources.

> ,, **When your body experiences problems it's worth finding out whether diet is contributing in some way and adjusting where necessary.**

Food intolerances are reported as being a common problem these days. If you're experiencing symptoms like bloating, headaches, stomachache or tiredness, it makes sense to investigate with a medical professional, or experiment with removing and adding different items from your diet. I suffered from a gluten intolerance that I was unaware of for years. The symptoms influenced my mood significantly. I remember being grumpy most of the time. It was like a breath of fresh air when I finally learned about the intolerance and made some dietary changes. Removing gluten from my diet changed my life and I've felt happier, more peaceful and pain free much of the time as a result. I'm sure this has made life easier for those I'm around too!

> ,, **Balancing the amount of food and drink we consume has a big impact on energy levels.**

We should take responsibility for our intake and diet to help maintain a steady flow of energy throughout the day. This helps keep the mind peaceful, which in turn helps us follow The Guidelines. I've experienced energy spikes from sugar quite a lot. A rush of energy just after eating a large slice of cake, followed by an energy dip a little while later. Caffeine has also played a big part in creating energy spikes, speeding up my thoughts and causing me to feel anxious. I significantly reduced my caffeine intake, which made a noticeable difference in energy regulation and most definitely contributed towards a more peaceful mind. When the body is in overdrive due to stimulants like caffeine and other drugs, our thoughts speed up. I appreciate that we all have different levels of sensitivities in these areas and that you need to make your own decisions about what's right for you.

Relaxation

The mind needs to be relaxed and alert to follow The Guidelines. To enable this, the body needs the same balance. Relaxation re-energizes the body. Our bodies are analogous to machines. They can't keep running constantly without down time. There are two types of relaxation. The first is planned relaxation, where you consciously decide to relax the body. Examples of this are laying down in corpse pose for a few minutes after physical yoga practice, having a relaxing massage or bringing awareness to different parts of your body. The second type of relaxation is spontaneous relaxation. This involves spontaneously relaxing the body during daily activities. Examples of this are keeping the body relaxed whilst typing on your computer or consciously relaxing your shoulders when you're standing in a queue.

> **Aim to combine both forms of relaxation, by integrating planned and spontaneous relaxation into your day.**

Regular planned relaxation enables more spontaneous relaxation. It's analogous to planned and spontaneous meditation. When we do our planned meditation regularly, we enhance our day-to-day activities by integrating a meditative state. It's like how working on a yoga pose in a class helps to improve your posture when you're involved in other activities. As with all things, everybody is different when it comes to their ability to relax. Relaxation has been a real challenge for me. My default states when I was younger were anxious and active. I needed to make a big effort to keep the body more relaxed. Exercise, yoga and meditation have been helpful companions. A good friend of mine is at the other end of the scale. He's the kind of guy that can relax anywhere for as long as he wishes. We're all different.

Exercise and movement are particularly helpful for relaxation, as they release tension we have stored in the body. Sometimes, it's necessary to exert the body before we relax. It can feel impossible to relax when we're too tense. This is why people who attend yoga classes will usually tell you how great they feel in the last few minutes of relaxation. This is because the body has released stored tension through the physical yoga and then been rewarded with proper relaxation. It feels wonderful!

As our body awareness increases we become more aware of tension and the need to relax. We learn to consciously relax the body if we're feeling anxious or tense. Once we relax the body we benefit from a relaxed mind. When my body has enjoyed enough relaxation, it notifies me when it's ready to start moving again. This happens if I have a snooze during the day. There will be a small charge of energy run through my body once it's finished resting, because it's ready to rise and carry on with activities. The same happens when it's time to rise in the morning. The body has an impressive way of notifying and guiding us without the need for conscious thought. When I relax for more than the body needs, my mind drifts off and does unhelpful things like craving or worrying. It's a sign that I should be doing something active and nourishing.

> **Yoga nidra is particularly good for relaxing the body and mind.**

It's a yoga practice that enables deep relaxation through guided instructions from a teacher, in person or via recorded audio. It helps you enter a super-relaxed state that lies between waking and sleeping. Awareness of different parts of the body and visualizations are used. There's an option of incorporating a personal intention within the practice. Because you're relaxed, this intention is lodged deep into the subconscious mind where it can be accessed in the background. This intention could be based on one of the guidelines. Whilst being deeply relaxed, you'll be programming your mind to follow The Guidelines. There are many good books and digital resources that cover yoga nidra. If you're interested in learning more, a good place to start is to read *Yoga Nidra*[6] by Swami Satyananda Saraswati. He's been responsible for making this practice more popular in the West over the last few years.

Proper relaxation has many benefits, including better quality sleep and stress reduction. Indirectly, it helps with weight management, as we're less likely to reach out for comfort food when we're less stressed. Relaxation also reduces anxiety, improves mood, boosts your memory and helps you to concentrate better. There are many studies that show how relaxation positively contributes towards your physical health, so it's an essential ingredient for honoring the body. It's wise to make planned relaxation a part of your daily practice. A few minutes of quality relaxation makes all the difference to your well-being.

Sleep

Sleep is another broad and well documented topic. Again, I'll keep this section brief and share a few useful pointers that I've collected over the years. I invite you to research each of these individual areas further as part of your own practice.

I read some interesting facts about sleep in an article by the BBC.[7] It references recommendations from specialists stating that adults should have eight hours sleep per night. Also, that under or over sleeping can lead to disorders in the areas of cognition, immune system, cardiovascular disease, glucose control and obesity. We all know how much better we feel when we're sleeping well. Here are a few ideas that helped me ensure I get the right amount of quality sleep:

1. Let go of using all digital devices at least fifteen minutes before sleep. Mobile phones, tablets and other devices stimulate the mind. Especially if they're internet-enabled and socially connected.
2. Meditate briefly before going to sleep. A simple breathing meditation for two minutes helps to relax you.
3. Perform a mental body scan just before sleeping by consciously bringing your awareness to each part of the body.
4. Practice gratitude before sleep, by recalling things you are grateful for. This will gladden the mind and contribute towards a more positive transition into sleep.
5. If it's noisy where you live and not possible to reduce the noise, then get yourself some comfortable ear plugs to use during sleep.
6. Select a peaceful alarm to wake you up in the morning rather than something abrupt or rowdy.
7. You spend much of your life asleep so it makes sense to ensure you have a good quality bed and mattress. Keeping the body comfortable during sleep is part of honoring the body.
8. Remove all clutter from your bedroom. Clutter in your external environment clutters the mind.
9. Allow fresh air into your bedroom during sleep if this is possible.
10. Avoid liquids at least three hours before sleep. This will help minimize the chance of your bladder waking you up during the night.
11. Let go of caffeine in the afternoon and evening. This will reduce mind stimulation.
12. Avoid foods which disturb your sleep and negatively influence your dreams. The foods I'm referring to here vary from person to person. For me, they tend to be spicy foods, cheese and chocolate. You'll need to experiment with this to see what helps and hinders your sleep.
13. Where possible, go to sleep and wake up at regular times. This will program your body and help you remain asleep for the duration.

14. Be mindful of how long you nap for during the day. If you do take a nap in the day, experiment with shortening its duration or removing it altogether. If we accept our tiredness during the day, we often find it soon passes. Observe how this positively impacts your sleep on an evening.

15. Analyze your sleep with a device. I used a wrist band to monitor the amount of light and deep sleep I was having. Deep sleep is where the mind stops dreaming and the body repairs and recharges. I noticed a big correlation between the amount of deep sleep I had and how well I felt the following day. The device monitored me overnight and fed the information to my phone and computer for review. You can analyze your sleep patterns and identify the things you do during the day that help or hinder your sleep quality.

Physical activity

The United Kingdom's National Health Service[8] offers physical activity guidelines for adults. It divides physical activity into aerobic and strength exercises. For the largest part of the population, between the ages of nineteen and sixty-four, the weekly aerobic recommendation is to take one of the follow two options or a mixture of both:

- At least two and a half hours of moderate aerobic activity - this includes things like brisk walking and cycling.
- At least one hour and fifteen minutes of vigorous aerobic activity such as running.

The recommendation implies that if you exercise vigorously, your body only needs half the amount of time you would need to spend doing non-vigorous exercise. The National Health Service also recommends that you intersperse light activity into long periods of sitting. In addition to this, strength exercises that work all major muscles are recommended at least twice each week.

> I recommend you review physical activity advice from a trusted source from time-to-time and make your own decisions about what's appropriate for you.

The reason I've shared the information above is to highlight approximately how much exercise is required. Unfortunately, many people fall way short of this and out of those people, a good proportion of them will have no idea of how much physical activity is required. Take the time to review where you are against what's recommended.

Personally, I enjoy combining running, walking and yoga, to ensure I'm ticking the boxes recommended here. I love physical activity. In particular, the endorphins released during running, enjoying nature during walking and using yoga to release tension and encourage body awareness. I've learned to work to an 'intelligent edge.' I'll challenge my body so that it causes discomfort, but not to the point where it causes sharp pain. Bodily discomfort during physical exercise helps you become fitter and stronger. Sharp pain during exercise is harmful and hinders progress with this guideline.

Generally speaking, the guideline "Do only what needs to be done" should be applied to physical activity. At its worst case, exercising excessively causes death or injury. On a subtler level, excessive exercise takes time and energy that's required to do other things to stay aligned. The intention should be to give your body just what it needs and establish the right balance.

Exercise addictions are common. I appreciate that in some cases, excessive exercising may be a healthier and tactical way to avoid a more harmful addiction. It's not sustainable though and at some point, the pain that's causing addictions must be faced, to enable full healing and restore balance.

Acceptance of the body

Part of honoring the body is acceptance of all the forms it takes. It's human nature to have preferences. You may have parts of your body that you're happy with and parts you'd like to change. Like everything else, the body changes. Even if we do get to a point where we're content with how we look, it doesn't last for long. Either our bodies or psychological preferences will change, leaving us dissatisfied and craving for things to be different. There's a whole spectrum of relationships that people have with their bodies from complete acceptance to complete resistance. Acceptance of the body leads to contentment, whilst psychological resistance of the body causes suffering. For most of us, we are usually somewhere in-between the two and will vary over time based upon the different conditions we experience.

Personally, I believe it's fine to do things to make the body healthy, strong and beautiful. This is part of honoring the body. But how do you know where to draw the line? How do you know when you're spending too much time at the gym or in the beauty salon? You ask yourselves two questions: The first is 'Am I causing myself or anybody else harm through influencing my body in this way?' Consider this question deeply. If the answer is yes, then what you're doing is unskillful and you should make changes. If the answer is no, then you move onto the next question: 'Is spending this amount of time and energy on the body preventing me from following The Guidelines?' If the answer is yes, then you should adjust your priorities. Excessiveness in exercise and any other area, always shows itself through a lack of balance and compromises elsewhere.

As you can imagine, analyzing these situations can be quite a task in more complex situations. You can feel your way through a situation like this. Even without thinking about The Guidelines, if they're being disregarded and you're aware of your body, you'll notice stress and uncomfortable feelings. On the positive side, if you're aware of your body and feeling OK about what you're doing, that will signal probable alignment with The Guidelines. This method of knowing through feeling can be used across all guidelines and situations. It's using your body to guide you, rather than depending purely on analysis through thought. We can only do so much with our limited conscious minds. Be careful not to be completely driven by your gut feelings though, as they may be leading you in the wrong direction. I like to use both the mind and the feelings in my body, to guide me and make decisions. When the two are in harmony I have complete faith and confidence in my actions.

There are two types of acceptance: Relative acceptance and absolute acceptance. Relative acceptance involves bringing acceptance to situations, people and concepts you form in your mind. Accepting you have a health problem or accepting the way a part of your body looks, is relative acceptance. Absolute acceptance on the other hand, is not about external things like the body or situations. And it's not about the past or future. Absolute acceptance is accepting your experience as it is now, in the present moment. Regardless as to whether it's pleasant, unpleasant or neutral. Absolute acceptance is really accepting our feelings about things, rather than accepting the things themselves.

Acceptance is very relevant to the body. It may feel like we're in resistance to a certain part of the body, an ache, a pain, or even a disease, when in fact, what we're resisting is one or more unpleasant feelings that are being triggered by the mind. We must work directly on accepting our feelings, in the present moment. Then, any subsequent action we take to influence our body positively, if indeed any action's required, will be skillful and aligned. The Guidelines can only be followed fully, once we've accepted our experience in the present moment. In order to accept things, we must be aware of them. We can't accept what we're unaware of. This is covered in more detail in the next chapter, "Be present, bringing awareness and acceptance into every moment." Body awareness techniques like the yoga nidra practice mentioned earlier, and meditation, all help to raise our awareness.

Energy

Your state of mind in any given moment directly influences your emotions, and whether you're being skillful. Your mind needs to be in balance to follow The Guidelines. If it's overly stimulated or anxious it will cease to function correctly. The mind also causes problems when it's dull and drowsy. We're looking for a sweet spot between the two extremes, where our mind is both relaxed and alert. I speak more about this in the following chapter, as it's related to awareness and acceptance. The reason it's so important to take responsibility for bodily energy is because mind and body are intrinsically connected. We support the mind by honoring the body.

There is always energy being channeled around the body.

> One of the easiest ways to feel energy in the body is to bring some awareness to your hands or feet.

They feel alive. The energy is often experienced as a tingling sensation, like a small electric current. Scientifically speaking, it is a form of electricity that pervades your entire body. The more body awareness you have, the subtler forms of energy you feel. I recall when my body came 'online.' I was overwhelmed to begin with, feeling all of this energy. I visited the doctor to see if I was suffering from blood pressure or some other illness – it turned out I wasn't. What happened is that through mindfulness and meditation training, my body awareness had risen. There had been energy flowing through my body all of the time; it's just that I hadn't felt it so intensely before. People are at different stages with feeling this energy. When I deliver mindfulness training, some people can feel the energy in most areas of their body. Others can't feel the energy at all. Turning the palms up, clenching the fists a couple of times, or curling your toes, helps intensify the sensations, making it easier to become aware of the energy.

Energy in the body is influenced through numerous factors including diet, intoxicants, sleep, emotions, confidence, stress, illness, allergies, physical activities, relaxation and exercise. We have to take responsibility for all of these things to ensure our bodily energy is balanced.

> **Keeping a journal for a few days helps raise the awareness of your energy levels.**

Log whether your energy has been low, balanced or excessively high, at regular intervals. Reviewing the events leading up to the time of an entry in the log will help you understand what you might need to change. Excessively high energy is unsustainable and leads to low energy at some point in the future. The body naturally regulates itself in this way.

There's an interesting link between activities we're involved in and energy levels within the body. Even something as simple as what we're watching on TV or the discussions we're having, has an impact. If we're doing something that's misaligned, our energy will be lowered at the time or lowered subsequently. The opposite is true in that when our activities are aligned, everything else being equal, our energy will feel balanced. The mind and the body contain the intelligence required to determine whether The Guidelines are being followed.

When we're misaligned, the mind experiences psychological stress and unpleasant feelings in the body. Whether we know about the stress manifesting will be dependent upon our level of awareness. If our awareness is low, the stress may pass unnoticed. The amount of psychological stress and unpleasant feelings we experience, is proportional to the degree to which we are misaligned. The impact of a slight misalignment will be subtle, as in the example of a relatively weak harmful thought passing through our mind with no further action being taken. A gross example of misalignment would be physically murdering another person. These two examples are at either end of the spectrum and therefore attract different levels of response from the mind and body.

Some people are so unaware that they never notice the psychological and bodily impact of their actions, even after a grossly misaligned act. This is often the case if people are severely ill – either physically or psychologically. Psychological and bodily impact can be experienced both during and after action is taken. The action I'm referring to here is thoughts, speech and physical action.

Alternative therapies may be explored as a way of enabling the flow of energy through the body. Strands of Hinduism, Yoga, Buddhism, Jainism and other traditions, use the concept of chakras. Chakras are claimed to be wheels of spinning energy that are part of the subtle body. The subtle body is described in some traditions as consisting of the spiritual constituents that make up the physical human body. Hindu teachings describe seven key chakras that run along the spinal cord. Some spiritual therapists claim to unlock energy blockages, thus allowing the energy to flow freely. Reiki healing is an example of this. There are various debates about if these practices really work or whether the effects of them are more to do with suggestion from the therapist. Either way, whatever helps people, so long as it's not causing harm and people are being truthful, will be aligned with The Guidelines, as ethical healing practices are acts of kindness.

Sexuality

You can review your sexuality using the three components of honoring the body: Prioritization, non-harm and nourishment. Firstly, you need to be aware of your sexual needs. You can do this by observing your bodily sensations, feelings and thoughts. I offer some guidance on this in the following chapter. Once you're tuned in to what your body needs sexually, you can allow for that in your priorities. How you do this will depend upon your individual situation. You may be perfectly happy with your sex life. It may mean a discussion with your partner, if you have an existing sexual relationship that you feel needs to change. If you're single, it may mean prioritizing the time and energy to find a partner, or finding other skillful ways of meeting your sexual needs. Some people are happy to be without a sexual partner or to let go of sexual activity altogether. The main thing is to be honest with yourself. Sexuality should never be continuously suppressed. Of course, there are times and places where sexual desires must be suppressed, in the spirit of kindness and non-harm. The energy will need to be released at some point though, so it's right to set up skillful ways of channeling it.

The second and third components of honoring the body, which are non-harm and nourishment, apply to sexuality. Non-harm in this context is referring to not harming your own body. Being kind to others, is covered in a separate guideline. Sexual activity either on your own or with others, should nourish your body. You'll know for yourself what this means in terms of frequency, intensity, duration and type of sex. When the body is nourished with sex, it leaves you feeling balanced and peaceful. If the body is harmed with sex you find yourself feeling intoxicated, exhausted or guilty. How you feel after sex says a lot about whether it was nourishing or harmful. Having sex when your body doesn't need it, either on your own or with others, is misaligned. It's actually stealing. Your mind is taking something from your body that it doesn't want to give. That's why it can feel so depleting afterwards. Manipulating others to have sex with you when they don't want to is also a form of stealing.

Non-harm means that we shouldn't frustrate our bodies. If we catch ourselves craving for sex that we cannot have at the time, or if it's inappropriate to have sex when we're craving, we should make a conscious effort to let go of any sexual thoughts and feelings, allowing the craving to pass. This is opposed to the unskillful route which is to fuel the cravings with fantasy or action. To stay aligned, sexual activity should respond to the needs of the body rather than reacting to the wants of the mind. Any sexual activity that is undertaken through psychological craving without a bodily need, can create an addiction and cause a depletion in energy.

> It's good practice to check in with yourself before engaging in sexual activity and ask whether your body really needs sex or whether sex is being pursued to avoid pain and suffering, which is a form of sexual addiction.

In extreme cases, excessive amounts of sex leads to physical or emotional exhaustion, making it impossible to follow The Guidelines.

Sexuality creates an abundance of energy within the body. Part of our awareness practice, which is covered in the next chapter, is to monitor sexual feelings and energy. Sexual energy needs to go somewhere and do something. When we take responsibility for our energy we can channel it. Energy from sexual impulses, often needs to be diverted away from the immediate goal of the body and towards something more skillful. It all starts with awareness. We become aware of the sexual feelings, we accept them, and then decide what appropriate action to take. The world would be in complete chaos if we all went around doing exactly what our bodies wanted!

Connections with other guidelines

All seven guidelines connect together and support each other. The table on the following page highlights a few of the connections between "Honoring the body" and the other guidelines.

Guideline	Connections
Be present, bringing awareness and acceptance into every moment	• This guideline, "Honor the body," can only be followed when you're present. • Accept the body including condition, shape, bodily sensations, feelings and general health. This places you in an aligned position to take positive action to change things if required. • Negative emotions deplete the energy within the body. Bringing acceptance to them helps them pass and conserves energy. • Awareness of energy within the body. • Awareness of bodily sensations and feelings. • Awareness of the position and posture of the body. • Awareness of the needs of the body. • Awareness of pleasure, discomfort and pain, within the body. • Bringing awareness and acceptance to every moment leads to a peaceful mind. This then naturally balances the energy in the body. • Awareness and acceptance of sexual energy allows it to be channeled skillfully.
Act with kindness, considering everyone and everything	• Being kind to the body. • Not harming yourself or others through excessive exercise or excessive beautification of the body. • Not stealing energy from the body by engaging in sex, when the body doesn't need it.
Understand the truth, communicating it selectively and skillfully	• Being honest with yourself in relation to your body. • Communicating bodily needs to others selectively and skillfully. • Consideration of body language within communication.
Do only what needs to be done	• Giving the body only what it needs, e.g. diet, exercise, sex, medication etc. • Using the body wisely and selectively.
Harmoniously obtain and retain only what you need	• Where possible, conditioning the body to allow it to meet the requirements of an aligned lifestyle. • Where possible, letting go of any excess weight that isn't required to meet The Guidelines.
Apply The Guidelines to your digital device usage	• Considering the impact of digital device usage on the body and adjusting where required, e.g. considering posture and eye strain. • Using digital information, products and services to help nourish, care for and protect the body.

You can find a list of ideas for practicing this guideline, in the final chapter "Building & Structuring Your Practice."

POINTS FOR REFLECTION

1. The body has a substantial influence over the mind. A healthy body helps the mind work effectively with The Guidelines.

2. Whatever state your body is in, you can always find ways to practice The Guidelines.

3. The body needs to be respected because it represents your part of The Process.

4. Prioritization means wherever possible, placing the genuine needs of the body first, above everything else.

5. Aches and pains in the body are often due to emotional problems and may eventually lead to disease if left untreated.

6. The mind needs to be relaxed and alert to follow The Guidelines. To enable this, the body needs the same balance.

7. It's wise to make planned relaxation a part of your daily practice. A few minutes of quality relaxation makes all the difference to your well-being.

8. Bodily discomfort during physical exercise helps you become fitter and stronger. Sharp pain during exercise is harmful.

9. One of the easiest ways to feel energy in the body is to bring some awareness to your hands or feet.

10. Excessively high energy is unsustainable and leads to low energy at some point in the future.

11. When our activities are aligned, everything else being equal, our energy will feel balanced.

12. When we're misaligned, the mind experiences psychological stress and unpleasant feelings in the body.

Be Present, Bringing Awareness and Acceptance into Every Moment

Stated negatively: Do not become lost in thought

I ADVISE YOU TO UNDERSTAND and practice all of The Guidelines. However, if you were only to focus on one of them, this is the guideline I'd recommend: "Be present, bringing awareness and acceptance into every moment" – the king of the guidelines. If you achieve mastery of this guideline, your application of all other guidelines will be mastered automatically. The body will be honored. You will be kind and truthful. You will only do what needs to be done. You will obtain and retain only what you need and your digital device usage will be spiritually perfected. This is why highly influential spiritual teachers place so much emphasis on being present.

Guideline: Be Present

Given this, you may be asking why you need to learn about the other guidelines if this one leads to mastery of them all. Interestingly, practicing the other guidelines makes it easier to follow this one. And practicing this guideline makes it easier to follow the others. This is analogous to sprinters building muscles in their legs by using different types of weight machines at the gym to help them run faster. Through running faster, their legs become stronger, making it easier to work with weights. These different practices support each other and work toward the same goal. This is true of all The Guidelines. The diagram at the start of this chapter shows how The Guidelines support each other with 'Be present' at the center.

Relationship with mindfulness and Mindfulness+

This guideline encourages us to be mindful in everything we do. There are many definitions for mindfulness. I define it as 'awareness and acceptance of bodily sensations, feelings and thoughts, within the present moment.' The diagram below illustrates a simplified version of these different components. In reality there are millions of them manifesting and interacting with each other. Our experience of what's manifested by The Process will always consist of bodily sensations including form coming in through the senses, feelings, and thoughts. I considered the option of simply calling this guideline 'be mindful' or 'be present.' Instead, I decided to expand the title to highlight that mindfulness is about acceptance as much as it is about awareness.

Mindfulness courses, books, and other resources are great. They help people reduce stress, manage pain, become more concentrated and offer a range of other benefits.

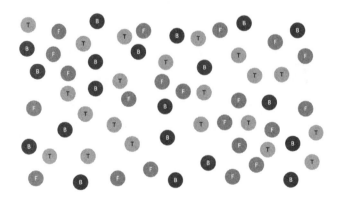

Components of Our Experience: Thoughts, Feelings and Bodily Sensations

> Exploring mindfulness teachings outside of what you find in
> this book will help you become more aligned.

This guideline provides mindfulness with an added bonus. The mindfulness
I practice, integrates the intelligence from The Process, also known as the
spiritual dimension. I call this Mindfulness+.

> When you're mindful and receptive to the intelligence within
> The Process, you receive much more than just standard
> mindfulness benefits.

This is why I add the plus. The spiritual dimension is the intelligence that
lies within The Process. When you're mindful and receptive to this infinite
intelligence or wisdom, your thoughts and actions are fully aligned with
The Guidelines. That's why this guideline is central to the others. Mind-
fulness+ is another name for this guideline. I'll help you understand more
about how all of this works through the introduction of a couple of models:
The Two Modes of the Mind and *The Four A's*.

The Two Modes of The Mind

Your mind is always in one of two modes. You're either lost in thought,
or you're present. Being lost in thought may also mean you're lost in your
emotions. During these times you're disconnected from the intelligence
of The Process. Instead, your ego is in control. When this happens, it
always leads to misalignment, even if only at a subtle level. When your
thoughts get carried away with themselves, without your awareness, they
create impressions in your mind that cause problems later. This is a form
of karma. Sometimes you can be lost in thought, and the misalignment
is more extreme. You end up saying or doing something very unskillful.
Unskillfulness always manifests from being lost in thought and misaligned
– misaligned with what The Process needs. Overall, The Process is going
in a positive direction of evolution. When you're lost in thought, and
unskillful, you're working against The Process – this is what causes stress.
It's fruitless and tiring – like swimming against an infinitely powerful
current. Working against The Process is psychologically fighting the whole
universe.

Being lost in thought is the same as being psychologically lost in the
realm of time. Our thoughts always operate within the realm of time.

They are either addressing the past or future. When we think in this way, without awareness, unpleasant feelings like resentment, sadness, anxiety, and worry are triggered within our bodies. Because being lost in thought also links to being lost in emotions, it leaves us feeling unpleasant. It's a human dysfunction that's necessary as we're evolving, and becoming more spiritually conscious.

The suffering created through this type of thinking is The Process's way of teaching us, and helping us evolve. It's providing correctional feedback. Once we have faith in The Process, we have faith in everything that happens. Nothing will worry us or cause us to be anxious. We will be aligned and at peace.

The only way you can be in alignment with what's happened, and what's to come, is through the present moment. This is practicing acceptance of everything. It's only from there can you think, communicate and act with real wisdom.

When you're lost in thought, the mind is unstable and you're trapped. Trapped in your ego, or the prison of your own mind. Action from this state of mind is limiting and restrictive. It's like a mobile phone without network coverage. Your mind can only act based on what it knows from its past experience without getting a live data feed from an infinite source. Be present, and get yourself connected.

We're moving away from being lost in thought, and towards being present, also known as Mindfulness+. These Two Modes of the Mind are shown in the diagram below along with their characteristics.

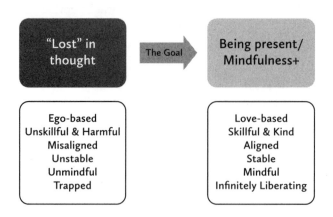

The Two Modes of the Mind

When you're present, your thoughts, communication and actions are automatically aligned and love-based. Love is a word that references the intelligence within The Process that connects and considers everyone and everything. This is what makes it possible to act with love and kindness. You're operating within the present moment and in tune with the needs of The Process. When the mind is in this stable state, The Process liberates you. You're free from the prison of your own ego, uncontrolled thoughts, and emotions. At one with everything that has been, everything that is now, and everything that's to come.

I must point out to you at this stage that it's OK to think! We need to think in order to do things and operate within the world. Thought that manifests out of a state of presence is skillful and helpful. That said, most of the time you don't actually need to think. Even when you're talking, you don't need to think. As I was writing this book I wasn't thinking most of the time. I was simply writing. If I was thinking too much and becoming lost in thought whilst writing, I wouldn't make any sense. I'm referring here to conscious thoughts. There are also subconscious thoughts in the background. As you work with this guideline and increase your awareness, it's possible to gain more access to your subconscious thoughts. You can view and investigate the background processes executed in your mind. These may be experienced as distant thoughts – little engines whirring away quietly.

When I'm peaceful I can identify the things my mind is working on behind the scenes. Not all of them – mainly those that are more prominent. All subconscious processes are part of The Process. They never disappear whilst your memory is operational. Everything leaves a trace. When the conditions are right, memories are resurrected, and old processes may execute within your subconscious or conscious mind. Each time a process is resurrected it takes on a different form because it's being influenced by new conditions. It's similar to a flower that disappears, and then pops out again the following year in a slightly different form, based on the weather and ground conditions at the time. We hold millions of these thought processes which increase in number based on our age, and the amount of stimulus we receive. This is the way I know things work based upon observing my own mind. Much of what I'm saying cannot be scientifically proven at this point in time. We have much to learn about the workings of our minds.

Operating systems on computers work in the same way and run background processes to keep things maintained. Users without knowledge of this don't even know that these processes are running. These users are analogous to people who don't understand what their subconscious minds are doing. You need to be equivalent to the skilled IT technician who knows how to view, stop and start the background processes in the computer. With time and practice, you'll gain deeper visibility and control over the conscious and subconscious parts of your mind.

Addictions take us away from being present. They use the subconscious mind for planning behind the scenes. The addiction is working away in the background, subconsciously planning for you to get or do whatever it needs. When you don't spot the addiction doing this you're its slave. An advantage of becoming more aware and observing your subconscious thoughts, is that you can spot your addictions in planning mode, ahead of when you might act. It's a great way of getting to know your addictions, and shedding light on them. This includes addictive thought patterns. Addictions loosen up, and are easier to work with when you bring awareness to them, including the subconscious elements.

There needs to be stillness and spaciousness within the mind. I'm sure you would have experienced this for yourself. Recall times when you were very present; when your mind was still and quiet. This happens naturally as we experience love or beauty. Some people experience this when they're out in nature, or keeping the body still. It can be experienced in challenging situations when we're under pressure. The mind becomes still, enabling us to say or do just what's required of us at the time. This is how people do remarkable things, make incredible decisions, and take action that literally transforms people and situations. Often our egos resurface after the event, and we might say to ourselves "That was impressive!"

99 **Observe the two modes of the mind in yourself and others.**

You can observe people and ask yourself if they're present or lost in thought. When they're lost in thought, whatever they say or do is unskillful and will cause harm. They will be misaligned with The Guidelines. Often, the more influence a person has, the bigger the impact based on their mode at the time. You don't know for sure what mode somebody else is in. You can only guess. However, it's a good observation game to play, which raises your awareness of the two modes of the mind.

Ultimately, the best person to observe in this practice is yourself. Human beings who are unenlightened, which is most of us, will have times when they're lost in thought and unskillful. For now, at this point in evolution, it's part of the human condition. By the way, enlightenment or awakening means being consistently aligned with The Guidelines – it is really the same thing.

> It can be helpful to ask yourself "Am I present?"
> When you ask yourself this question you automatically
> become present.

In fact, you need to be present to even ask yourself the question in the first place. If you have friends that understand this guideline then you can ask each other. Especially at times when one notices the other is lost in thought, or unskillful. Similar questions include, "Are you here?", "Are you with us?" or "Were you present when you did that?" Certain group activities lend themselves to being more present. I run spiritual study groups where we practice being present together whilst studying and communicating. It doesn't take a rocket scientist to work out the kind of activities that cause you to be present, and those that cause you to be lost in thought!

> Engage in more activities where you can be present,
> and fewer activities where you are lost in thought.

Bringing awareness to something real like the energy in your hands, or another part of the body, is a good tactic to regain presence. Or use your senses by looking around, listening, smelling, tasting or touching. When you do this, you become present. You may want to take a moment now to stop reading, and reflect on what it's like to be lost in thought. When was the last time this happened to you and how did it negatively impact things? Then take another moment to reflect on what it's like to be present. When was the last time this happened to you and how did it positively impact things?

To summarize, the mind is either lost in thought or Present. The goal is to become more present, and it's achievable for us all. Maybe just for small periods to begin with. Working with this guideline is at least a lifetime's work for most of us. We keep practicing, and over time we see quite how far we've come. We look back a few months or years, and are wowed by how much progress we've made. By studying The Guidelines, and practicing them, we move forward.

The Four A's

To help you bring awareness and acceptance to every moment I'd like to introduce a second model to you called The Four A's. It builds on the previous model by introducing acceptance and resistance. This is a useful way of describing the flow of mindfulness+ and its subsequent action.

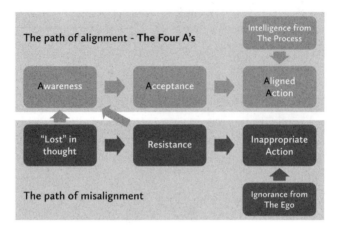

The top path in the diagram, the path of alignment, is what you need to be following. This links very much to mindfulness practice. It starts with awareness. You're aware of the present moment, or a particular situation. The next step is to bring acceptance to what you're aware of. From there, you'll always take aligned action. This is the path of the Four A's: **A**wareness, **a**cceptance, and **a**ligned **a**ction. This path is in alignment with The Process. Even if you've never heard about The Guidelines, when you follow this path you'll always align yourself with them.

The bottom path is the path of misalignment, which should be avoided. When we're lost in thought, we're resisting our experience in the present moment. Being lost in thought is a form of dreaming. Instead of being aware and accepting of what's taking place inside and around us, we drift off into uncontrolled thought. When this happens, we lose touch with our direct experience. As I've already mentioned, any thoughts that we experience, and subsequent action from this state will be misaligned, causing harm to ourselves and others. This misalignment is rooted in ignorance from our ego. The ego wishes to control situations to accommodate its own fear-based agenda rather than wanting what's good for The Process in its entirety. The ego can be forgiven for this, given its lack of connection to the intelligence within The Process. It's analogous to somebody doing something wrong because they don't know better. When we experience suffering, it's feedback from The Process, and an instruction to switch from the path of misalignment, to the path of alignment.

Fortunately, we can intervene when we're lost in thought or in resistance. If we have enough awareness to catch ourselves on the wrong path, we can regain awareness and switch to the right path. Switching paths in this way is empowering, and gets easier with practice. You may be able to recall a time when you've done this. Maybe when you stopped yourself saying or doing something unskillful. You caught yourself in a state of resistance just before you were about to say or do something, and corrected yourself before any external harm was caused.

What's actually happening here is that The Process is aligning you through your active connection to it. You may also recall times when you've been in a dream-like state. Uncontrollably craving for something that you wish to have or achieve. Or creating stories in your mind about situations and people that may not be true. When you catch yourself doing this, you can creatively shift to a more positive state of mind.

> **Switching from the path of misalignment to the path of alignment can be enabled through physical action, in addition to psychological action.**

When conditions are challenging, it can seem impossible to become aware and accepting through simply deciding to do so, or waiting for feelings to pass. Especially if powerful emotions have been invoked when you're lost in thought. In these cases, it may be worth distracting yourself for a while from the chain of thought and emotions. Maybe by engaging in a different activity, or doing something physical like taking a walk. A change in your physical state and mindset helps you become present again. Then, once you're present, if you do need to return to an activity or situation where you were lost in thought previously, you can do so from a fresh mental position where you're starting again positively and peacefully.

Another option is to sit and wait patiently until the stream of difficult emotions and unskillful thoughts pass. When you observe unpleasant feelings without distracting yourself, some or all of the pain associated with them gets released. This is the process of healing.

People ask me about daydreaming and the part that plays in creative processes. We often birth beneficial ideas when the mind's daydreaming.

My response is to allow the daydreaming to initially come from a state of awareness. And to finish in a state of awareness. This means that you'll only be daydreaming when and where it's skillful to do so. For example, when you're resting on a couch and nothing needs your attention you may 'choose' to daydream. Daydreaming is unskillful when it takes place unconsciously at times when you need to be aware; like when you're listening to somebody or walking across a busy road. It's analogous to allowing small children to play freely and do whatever they wish for a while – it's good for them. However, responsible parents only allow their children to do this in a safe environment and at an appropriate time.

Dealing with emotional pain

I remember visiting the beach for a few hours on a warm spring afternoon. I felt some frustration and emotional uncomfortableness as I was walking there. After sitting for a while, I became aware of unpleasant feelings being triggered by emotions. In parallel, I observed my mind trying to escape from them. First it was craving for caffeine. Then, my mind craved for potato chips, and finally ice cream. I didn't consume any of these things. Instead, I just sat with the cravings and emotional pain for a little while. After a few minutes, it passed, as all things do. The whole process was certainly challenging and painful, whilst at the same time, it felt super-empowering. It gives me confidence; every time I can rise above emotional pain in this way. I know that through doing this I'm allowing the pain to heal. On reflection, I should have treated myself afterwards to a coffee, potato chips and ice cream as a reward for being with my feelings!

The easy option would have been to go for the pleasure and succumb to the cravings. That's how most people dodge emotional pain. Me included sometimes. The first problem with doing that, is that you fail to give the pain the awareness it needs to leave your body. You continue to carry that pain with you, along with the fear that goes with it. The second problem, is that whenever you escape from pain in this way, you create addictions. The mind creates a link between the feelings associated with the pain, and the feelings associated with whatever activities you select as the escape route. The next time you experience the pain, it's likely that you'll be inclined towards the same escape route. In the example I provided, it would have been caffeine, salty food or sugary food. Addictions are much wider than this and can include all sorts of activities including repetitive and unhelpful thought patterns.

Sometimes I'll physically moan when I'm accepting intense emotional pain. It's an uncomfortable business. If I'm experiencing extreme feelings of anger, I might whack a cushion to release the energy from my body. It's never caused me any harm, and I haven't heard of anybody else who have harmed themselves through this practice. In fact, it's a form of kindness as it's only through accepting emotional pain in this way that we can reduce and release it.

The yogis have been practicing this for centuries in the form of Tapas or the burning of karma. Satchidananda[3] talks about being grateful to people who trigger pain within you. These people are your ego's perceived enemies. Jesus told his followers to love their enemies. You need people and situations to trigger pain, so that you can heal, and release it from your body. Otherwise, it remains dormant and you continue carrying it around with you.

When I meet new people, they often tell me I look happy, and believe that I'm like that all of the time. I'm not. There are plenty of times when I experience emotional pain and unhappiness. During these times I look quite unpleasant or unwell. The reason I'm happy most of the time is that I make a conscious effort to let go of emotional pain within my body. As soon as is practically possible. Nature is a real help. I often take emotional pain to nature. I walk or sit where I find trees, grass, flowers or beautiful views. It feels like nature is extracting the pain from me and absorbing it.

It works the other way around too. Sometimes, I'll go into nature without even knowing I have emotional pain – I'll be repressing it. And then, just through being there, pain is released from my body. Firstly, nature brings the emotional pain to my attention. Then, nature extracts and absorbs it. Nature can be used as a gateway for you to access the intelligence within The Process. This intelligence then guides your consciousness towards any emotional pain, and gives you the faith to accept it. Emotional pain needs to be acknowledged and accepted before it can be released. This is all part of healing. Nature heals.

People ask me how to deal with regular intense and unpleasant feelings. There are four options I recommend, which I've listed below. The first two are reactive; they may be applied whilst the feelings are being experienced. The third and fourth options are more proactive; they may be applied at times when the feelings are not being experienced.

1. Bring full awareness to the feeling in the way that I described earlier.
2. Change your physical state. Go for a walk, displace yourself. Do a simple physical activity.

3. Where possible, change your conditions to minimize the chances of that feeling being triggered in the future. For example, if the feeling is triggered when you view somebody's social media feed, then let go of viewing it.

4. Work with a wise friend or a good therapist to explore the root cause of the unpleasant feelings.

These four options enable you to take responsibility for the unpleasant feelings. Even if somebody else triggered them, they're your feelings, so you're responsible for them until your pain is healed.

I apply this practice whenever possible, rather than dodge the pain by distracting myself with something pleasurable. Another tactic the ego likes is to escape from painful feelings by triggering different painful feelings, which are often more intense. This is how we negatively spiral downwards and exhaust ourselves. Release yourself from this cycle by being very aware and accepting of emotional pain when it arises.

> **Actively healing old emotional pain should be a central part of your practice.**

This type of healing reduces the emotional pain you carry inside your body, making it less likely to disturb your balance and peacefulness in the future.

The pain-body

In his book *The Power of Now*, Eckhart Tolle[1] discusses the pain-body. The pain-body is a useful concept which helps you practice this guideline. My understanding of the pain-body, is that it's an accumulation of old emotional pain that's built up over the years, including from previous lives. I view it as a concept; a changeable process – not something that's fixed. When emotions from the pain-body are activated, we become lost in thought and misaligned. It can even manifest in a subtle form like when we experience a quick, passing unpleasant feeling. Its significant manifestations can leave us feeling terrible for hours or even days. If you have a high level of body awareness, you can feel the pain-body activating in the form of unpleasant feelings.

As a tactic, it can help to view your pain-body as an enemy of The Process, as it appears to do its best to try and stop you from evolving. The truth is that the pain-body, and everything else, is a creation of The Process. The Process creates all sorts of things and situations that appear 'bad' in the eyes of our egos, when these creations are actually all part of something much bigger than us, which is a positive process of evolution. This process of evolution will ultimately lead to the extinction of human beings. Everything is created, sustained and destroyed. How can we credibly say that humans must survive forever when we don't understand the entirety of The Process? It's human nature and the role of the ego to want to sustain what The Process has made us a part of. Anything can seem 'bad' without the wider perspective. This wider perspective is only available from the intelligence within The Process. This full perspective cannot be analyzed with the mind or communicated in traditional ways. It can only be known.

Personally, I've found the concept of the pain-body extremely useful in my practice. I watch it activate within my body, and then become dormant again, just as Tolle describes. When I'm experiencing unpleasant feelings, I say to myself "My pain-body is active." This then creates a space between my true Self, and the pain-body. A shift in awareness takes place, and I'm once again back in the present moment and on the path of alignment.

You may spot the pain-body arising in other people. Friends who understand the pain-body can kindly acknowledge it activating in each other. When somebody does this for you it helps you shift perception and regain awareness. I believe the pain-body disappears for good once all of your emotional pain has been released. This happens through full and consistent alignment with The Guidelines.

Most of my pain-body occurrences over the years have been through pain I've stored in my body from a troubled and anxious childhood. During a therapy session, I was telling the therapist about the way I react in certain situations. Giving him details about what I was thinking, and how I was feeling. He said, "That's the child in you, Darren." In a way he was right. The unpleasant feelings were triggered from pain stored within me from childhood. When the pain-body was active, the feelings triggered childlike thoughts. It felt the same as when I was experiencing the pain as a child. If I communicated with others at the time, whilst the pain-body was active, I'd even sound like a child. Links between the feelings and thoughts were still there after all those years. In discussion with friends and people who I train, I've noticed the majority of pain-body occurrences are related to things that happen during childhood. It's very common. This is where a good therapist can be helpful, as they work with you to extract the pain, and then help you to reduce or let go of it. They may not know it, but many therapists are operating as pain-body reducers.

For most of us, we have to accept that when we're feeling OK, the pain-body has not disappeared, but is dormant like a sleeping animal that can wake up and cause us problems in the form of triggering painful feelings. These problems are actually opportunities to heal if we can stay present and allow them to pass. Sadly, at times when the pain-body takes over our minds, so to speak, we only regain our awareness after thinking, communicating, or acting in a way that's misaligned. The positive to be acknowledged here, is that the suffering this creates can help wake us up, and motivate us to be more present in the future. Suffering is a great teacher. We must be vigilant and aware, even at times when the pain-body is dormant, when our feelings are neutral or pleasant. The earlier we can be aware of pain-body manifestations, the easier it is to transcend them. The pain-body doesn't like awareness; it feels threatened by it. Ultimately, it's our awareness that kills the pain-body in the same way that sunlight kills vampires.

Relative acceptance

To help you become more accepting, you start by accepting there are two forms of acceptance: Relative acceptance and absolute acceptance. Relative acceptance is conceptual. For example, your mind believes you need to bring acceptance to a situation or a person. It may be that your property is damaged by a storm, or a friend is behaving in a way that you think is unkind. These are conceptual situations. We need to accept them at that same conceptual level, through thought.

When we're in resistance to situations like these, the resistance is actually a story we're creating in our minds. In the example about the property, the story might be, "This shouldn't be happening to me. I don't deserve this. I blame the person for not fixing the roof properly the last time this happened." It causes psychological suffering. The mind then triggers unpleasant emotions within the body. The stories and emotions are the two components of your ego. The psychological or thinking component, and the emotional component. These two components are partners in crime. They work together to cause as much suffering as they can when we're lost in thought. Eventually, our awareness shines through and the suffering stops, at least for a while, until the ego is triggered again.

Emotional complaining is a form of resistance and reactivity. You complain about a person or situation, and experience unpleasant feelings like anxiety, anger or frustration. This may be complaining in person, over the phone, through messaging or within your own mind. In these instances, the complaining feels stressful and drains you of energy. The frequency of emotional complaints made by a person is inversely proportional to their general awareness and level of alignment. The more somebody emotionally complains, the less evolved they are. Emotional complaining is always a sign of resisting The Process. Prolonged resistance leads to exhaustion.

> Be kind to yourself. Be kind to your body. Practice acceptance.

Emotional complaining is different to conscious complaining. When you consciously complain about something, you do so without being overwhelmed by unpleasant feelings at the same time. For example, if your flight is delayed and you arrive at your destination significantly later than expected, it's fine to make a complaint. The service you received is different to what you paid for and expected. You can only complain consciously when you're accepting a situation. If you complain from a state of resistance, the complaining will be emotional and negative. If you were to complain about the flight from a state of acceptance, you'd speak or write to the agent with a peaceful mind. Your communication would be calm and kind. This would make your whole experience stress free and make life easier for the agent. It's for this reason that conscious complaining usually yields more favorable results than emotional complaining.

Acceptance of these situations is called relative acceptance. The resistance we experience is relative resistance, which is a form of craving. We genuinely believe that things should have turned out some other way, and we're craving for our ego's agenda to be met. The stress is caused because what's happened cannot be different. Once things are done they're done. The Process cannot be undone or reversed. Certainly not by us. It is not as though Superman can fly around the world in the opposite direction to which it's spinning and turn back time! If we're all part of some computer simulation as I discussed earlier, you could claim that somebody or something may be able to press the rewind button and change things in the past. Even if this were to happen, or does happen, we wouldn't know about it so we should always come back to the practice of acceptance. Stress is a psychological argument about what is, between you and The Process. Through its truthfulness, The Process always wins these arguments.

How do we bring acceptance to situations our ego finds difficult? How can we practice relative acceptance? Over time, circumstances change. In the example of the friend who you believe is unkind, they may change at a later date, and become kinder. If you're happy with them, you may forget about your previous resistance and move on from there. This isn't practicing acceptance. The conditions change and the resistance passes automatically. When this happens, you're always at risk of future suffering. The resistance doesn't completely pass. It lays dormant within your mind. Everything is stored. If it happens again, or when you bring the previous incident to mind, the psychological and emotional suffering is triggered, and the pain returns.

Personal relationship breakups often provide illustrations of this. You can separate from your partner who you believe has been unskillful towards you, and even let go of all communication with them in an attempt to break free from the suffering. If the pain associated with past resistance you've experienced hasn't been fully accepted, you may continue to experience it at a later date when The Process provides the triggers. It provides the triggers to give you another opportunity to accept the pain. The pain is stored within the body, and surfaces from time to time until it's healed. When The Process triggers emotional pain within you, it's giving you an opportunity to heal it. With this in mind you can view the manifestation of emotional pain as helpful.

Relative acceptance is about coming to terms with concepts in your mind. It's about rationalizing situations so that you can accept them on a conceptual level. This type of acceptance doesn't reduce the emotional pain you carry around with you. However, it can allow you to move forward, as your psychological functioning eases in relation to what you've accepted. In the property example above, you may accept that the person who fixed your roof previously, did the best job they could at the time, and accept the difficult weather conditions that caused the damage. You may psychologically come to terms with what happened in the broken relationship example, by understanding the conditions that caused your ex-partner to behave the way they did.

Relative acceptance is useful in dealing with situations we're resisting. Resistance reduces over time through practicing The Guidelines. Resistance to situations is due to attachments. Our ego attaches to all sorts of things including roles, assets, opinions, beliefs, stories, relationships and habits. Attachments prevent us from being truly creative in the moment. The ego feels threatened when conditions from The Process work against what it believes it consists of. For example, if you're identified with a relationship and that relationship is threatened, the ego resists the situation. It fears losing the relationship, so creates stress and a barrage of negative thoughts and unpleasant emotions as a way of trying to control the situation. The ego fears its own destruction. Spiritual practice and alignment are about destroying the ego, which is why it gets stressed. The ego's stress can feel like your stress. It's not your stress. It's the ego's stress, that you have to take responsibility for.

Relative resistance is the negative opposite state to relative acceptance. It's when you're resisting a situation. I do a lot of my writing in cafés in the UK. I often observe people complaining about the cost of their food and drink. It seems to be a cultural pastime for many in the UK to emotionally complain about the price of things. People purchase food and drink, and then get annoyed afterwards, complaining about how much they've paid for it! This is an example of relative resistance. A great opportunity for them to practice acceptance.

You need the concept of time to practice relative acceptance. It requires thought, because thought is associated with past or future. Relative acceptance requires you to analyze a situation and come to terms with it in your mind. Understanding the truth helps – more on that in Chapter Six. Relative acceptance is only partial acceptance. The only way you can truly free yourself from emotional pain, and become fully aligned, is through the practice of absolute acceptance…

Absolute acceptance

Absolute acceptance, which is what we practice through mindfulness, transcends time and situations. It's not about the past or future. It's about accepting your direct experience as it is now in the present moment – a real-time activity, regardless of whether the experience is pleasant, neutral or unpleasant. Absolute acceptance is accepting our thoughts, feelings, bodily sensations, and stimulus coming in through the senses, within the present moment. This is different to relative acceptance, which is psychologically accepting situations in time, through thought. Relative acceptance is largely a psychological practice whilst absolute acceptance is more instinctive.

Emotional pain we experience gets stored physically, which is why absolute acceptance is the only thing that enables true healing. Absolute acceptance is the ultimate form of acceptance, and requires no thought. Every moment is accepted. Once we've mastered absolute acceptance, the need for relative acceptance drops away. The reality for most of us as we evolve, is that we'll need to practice a combination of relative and absolute acceptance.

What's wonderful about absolute acceptance is that you can bring it all back to yourself, and your own practice. With absolute acceptance you aren't dependent upon external conditions being a certain way that suits your ego's desires and aversions. You can be free from psychological suffering regardless of what happens to you or around you. There are no dependencies on past or future. When you're absolutely accepting your experience, even the events leading up to your own death will not create psychological suffering. A genuine and full absence of the fear of death is a sign of significant spiritual progress. This proves that an individual really knows the workings and intention of The Process, regardless of whether they can articulate it. Absolute acceptance provides you with real confidence and spiritual power.

I can't guarantee that everything will be pleasant for you if you follow this practice, as The Process doesn't guarantee that. Take the story of Jesus being tortured on the cross, or the Buddha dying of food poisoning. The scriptures claim these men were fully awakened – so they would have been aligned with The Guidelines. Even Jesus and the Buddha would have experienced unpleasant feelings in their bodies. You can't escape them, but you can escape being lost in thought, which for most of us constitutes the vast majority of our suffering. In my experience, when you align with The Guidelines, and practice absolute acceptance, everything else being equal, you experience fewer unpleasant feelings in the body. This is due to you reducing the psychological suffering that triggers them. Reducing psychological suffering reduces bodily suffering. The two are linked. People that experience stress, which is what psychological suffering is, will often experience physical aches, pains, illness and disease. In extreme cases it can even lead to a person's death. If you follow The Guidelines, the chances are that you'll live longer – now there's motivation to practice!

Each moment of absolute acceptance signifies a moment of complete faith in The Process. Because the moment is accepted, everything before and after it, is also being accepted. Without this, you experience feelings like resentment and anxiety. An indication of absolute acceptance is a peaceful mind. No psychological suffering is present during this time. No negative thoughts. The reward for complete faith in The Process is peace. The intelligence within The Process can also be described as peace. You can say that peace is its own reward.

So how can absolute acceptance be practiced? How is it possible to accept everything that enters your awareness? The first step *is* awareness. You need to be aware of something before you can accept it. When I'm delivering mindfulness training it's common for people to ask me how to practice acceptance. I explain about the difference between relative and absolute acceptance, and then suggest they focus on awareness. The miracle, is that when awareness is present, acceptance automatically follows. Absolute acceptance then becomes instinctive. Remember, I'm not referring to acceptance of situations here. I'm talking about acceptance of your experience within a given moment. Bodily sensations, form coming in through the senses, feelings and thoughts.

Identifications and the ego

Staying present and accepting our experience is highly influenced by our identifications, also known as attachments. Our minds identify with all sorts of things including possessions, knowledge, relationships, roles, likes, dislikes, beliefs, creations, opinions, resentments, appearances, positive or negative comparisons, addictions, attachments from the past, and fantasies about the future. When you add all of your identifications together, you get the ego, or your false sense of self. When your mind is lost in thought, your ego takes over, which means that one or more of your identifications is being utilized. The larger your ego, the more potential you have to be lost in thought.

The size of your ego is a factor of the number of identifications, and the depth to which they are ingrained in the mind. The more identification-based thought patterns are repeated, the larger the imprint on the ego. It's also true to say that most of the time, the deeper the identification, the more challenging it is to reduce or release it.

> If you find yourself lost in thought, it can be helpful to reflect on what you've been thinking, and to work out which identifications were being utilized at the time.

This will shed light on your identifications, and therefore your ego. Awareness reduces the ego. That's why the ego dislikes it! One of the things I love about meditation is that it highlights my identifications. The things I'm identified with most strongly trigger most of the unhelpful emotions and thoughts. I find there are usually between three to five identifications or common themes that cause the bulk of the distractions. They change from time-to-time, based on what's going on in my life.

> See if you can determine your identifications. The things that cause you to become lost in thought.

Knowing your triggers makes it much easier to bring yourself back into awareness, and avoid getting into situations that may lead to you becoming lost in thought.

Becoming more aware

Being present is all about awareness and acceptance. You can only accept your experience when you're aware of it. Acceptance naturally flows from awareness. This guideline, "Be present, bringing awareness and acceptance into every moment," is the king of The Guidelines. If you were only to actively practice one guideline, it should be this one. Similarly, when you look within this guideline it contains one element that's more important than any other – awareness. With awareness, you open yourself up to the benefits of acceptance, and a connection with the infinite intelligence provided by The Process, that will guide you well. Awareness is critical to any spiritual practice.

I'd like to explain what I mean by awareness. I'm referring to awareness of form. By form, I mean bodily sensations, things coming in through the senses, feelings and thoughts. This is your *direct awareness*. I'm not referring to *conceptual awareness*, which is awareness of situations and concepts you create in your mind. Here are some examples of direct awareness:

- Being aware of the energy within your hands.
- Feeling warmth from the sun on your face.
- Awareness of thoughts.
- Recognizing a feeling of excitement.
- Hearing the engine of an airplane.

And here are some examples of conceptual awareness:

- Knowing that your laptop battery is about to die.
- Keeping in mind that your friend will be visiting within the next hour.
- Anticipating that a bird you're looking at will fly away if you move too hastily.
- Deducing your child is upset because they're tired from a busy day.
- Deducing that it's been raining outside because there are puddles on the ground.

Do you understand the difference between the two types of awareness? Direct awareness requires no discursive thought or interpretation of your experience. It's concerned with the present moment. Conceptual aware-ness on the other hand, does have some mental commentary or dialogue attached to it. And because thought is involved, time is also involved. Con-ceptual awareness is always about the past or future in some way.

It's ironic that in this day and age, most of us have been offered no train-ing in awareness. Fortunately, things are starting to change now with the gradual inclusion of things like mindfulness and yoga training at schools, but there's a long way to go. The same goes for listening. Children learn all sorts of things in school and from their parents that they'll never need, but most of them have no formal training in some of the basic life skills.

Even without any formal training, people find themselves at different levels when it comes to awareness. The level of somebody's awareness is dependent upon a multitude of conditions including their health, genetics, and past conditioning from earlier in life, and possibly previous lives. Practicing awareness is similar to practicing any of The Guidelines. Your ability to be aware is influenced by your conditions at the time including your health, the environment, people you're in communication with, and the activities you're involved in.

Cultivating awareness

Awareness is similar to physical strength. If you find yourself in an emer-gency situation it's surprising quite how much strength you find. Especially if you're protecting your own life, the lives of loved ones, or things that are dear to you. We hear stories about people who have lifted extraordinary amounts of weight in order to free somebody who has been buried due to an earthquake, or people who have the stamina to cling onto the side of a mountain for hours while they wait to be rescued. The faculty of awareness is similar to this. When we're in emergency situations our awareness is heightened significantly. I experience this if I'm at risk of being in a car accident. Whenever I enter a dangerous situation on the road, my aware-ness becomes intense without consciously trying. It's as though something more powerful than my conscious thoughts takes over and protects me.

Awareness is also similar to physical strength in that it cannot be trans-formed overnight. You can't go from being weak to strong through one session at the gym. In the same way, generally speaking, you can't go from having low awareness to consistently high awareness simply by reading a mindfulness book or doing a single meditation session. Awareness is culti-vated over time. Fortunately for us, awareness can be transformed through practice. Even within the space of a few weeks you can see a positive differ-ence. Often, people's awareness increases naturally through the aging pro-cess and life experiences without the need for any formal spiritual practice.

Awareness may be transformed through tragic life events or periods of great suffering. In his book *The Power of Now*,[1] Eckhart Tolle claims to have awakened after a period of intense suffering, and many similar cases of transformational uplifts in awareness have been evidenced. Steve Taylor's book, *The Leap*,[9] helpfully explains more about the awakening process, and the different journeys that people take. Our awareness increases every time we let go of identifications. Through doing this we are reducing the ego. The level of our awareness is inversely proportional to the size of our ego. The smaller the ego, the greater our awareness. The ego is like a veil that blocks our ability to observe what's going on, drawing us into unhelpful thoughts.

I was largely identified with a corporate career for many years. One day, I entered the office as per usual, and was told that I had to pull together my belongings and leave within twenty minutes. A number of us were made redundant and lost our jobs this way. I recall my ego causing me to feel embarrassed, small and very anxious. My family depended upon me for financial support. I was scared about what might happen if I were unable to quickly find another job. I left the office and drove home. As I approached my home, for the first time I spotted colored fields spanning the horizon at the end of my road. I'll never forget how beautiful they were. The shock from the redundancy, and space created in my mind through the severed identification, allowed me to bring more awareness to my surroundings. It was a profound experience. As it happened, within the space of a couple of weeks, I was offered a more enjoyable job where I was needed. It's often the case that when something is taken from you, you go on to obtain a more suitable substitute.

For most of us, our increase in mindfulness will be gradual. The devel-opment in mindfulness through the aging process, and our life experience, may be accelerated through spiritual practice. The Yoga Sutras claim that the more intense our practice, the quicker we progress. I can relate to this. I'm confident that the vast majority of my own increase in awareness has been a result of spiritual practice. I don't claim to be awakened, but I do claim to have made great progress from my starting position in childhood, and early adulthood. I was sadly lacking in awareness, and led a broadly unskillful and stressful life as a result of that. I'm not perfect now by any stretch of the imagination, but the progression over the years and peace of mind I've obtained has been tremendous thanks to spiritual practice. I know this wouldn't have been possible without meditation, the study of spiritual texts, yoga, spiritual friendship, reflection, and healing emotional pain through acceptance.

There are many ways you can cultivate awareness. I'll share a few with you that I know about and have experienced for myself. This is by no means an exhaustive list. I encourage you to try some of these practices. I also encourage you to explore other ways of increasing your direct awareness through research or experimentation.

Setting up a regular meditation practice will most certainly improve your awareness.

> **In terms of practice, the first option I recommend is simply sitting without concentrating on anything in particular.**

Bring awareness to the different components of your experience: bodily sensations, form coming in through the senses, feelings and thoughts. This meditation can be practiced wherever you are. To begin with, it helps to practice in places where there are fewer distractions. If you find yourself lost in thought, then simply bring your awareness back to the breath, and then begin again, widening your awareness to everything you're experiencing. I find this type of meditation pleasurable as it gives the mind a break from thinking. It's relaxing as you simply sit and be.

> **Another meditation approach that lends itself well to raising awareness is to systematically cycle around the different aspects of your experience.**

Start with your bodily sensations, moving onto things coming in through the senses, followed by your feelings, and then finally, your thoughts. You can spend a few minutes on each section.

> **Maintaining awareness on your breath will keep you grounded whatever activity you're involved in.**

Being aware of your breath connects you to something that's real, rather than thought-based. During your daily activities you can keep a small percentage of awareness on the breath, maybe ten percent, with the rest of your awareness open to observe what's presented to you. If you find this difficult during daily activities then train yourself with a breathing-based meditation. When you're aware of your breath more consistently in meditation, you'll find it easier to do the same outside of meditation.

I introduced yoga nidra practice in the third chapter as a way of relaxing the body.

> Through practicing yoga nidra you'll be increasing your awareness and relaxing the whole body in parallel.

You have the option of using the list of seven guidelines as intentions at the start and end of the yoga nidra session. This will install The Guidelines deep into your subconscious mind, making it easier to recall and integrate them within daily activities.

> The physical practice of yoga, also known as asana, increases body awareness whilst helping build strength and flexibility.

Good yoga teachers encourage you to maintain awareness of your breath and body throughout a yoga session. I've practiced yoga for many years and the benefits are incredible. I found it really challenging to begin with. My mind created suffering through comparison with others. Once I let go of that, and focused on the yoga, rather than my own ego, the whole practice lightened up and became pleasurable. Even today, after years of practice, I thoroughly enjoy every session. I don't do the complicated postures. Instead, I opt for a basic and balanced sequence, which I vary from time-to-time. I mainly practice at home in solitude and go to classes occasionally to learn more and practice with others.

Flexible and strong yoga experts do incredible things with their bodies. Yoga can be an art form. The key point to yoga practice in relation to The Guidelines is that it builds strength, flexibility and most importantly, awareness. If you have those three elements, you'll be setting yourself up nicely regardless of whether you can wrap your legs around the back of your head! Attending a beginner's yoga class or retreat is a great way of getting started.

There's another link between the body and awareness, relating to posture. If possible, keep your back, neck and head in a straight line whilst you meditate. This helps you remain alert and allows energy to flow freely through the body. Poor posture or slouching, acts as a hindrance to awareness. It may encourage you to become sluggish and lost in thought. I appreciate that some people cannot maintain a straight posture due to health reasons and physical limitations. It's possible to be aware without a straight posture, just more challenging.

> **If you're capable of maintaining a straight posture then it makes sense to do so. Not just within meditation, but whenever you need to stay aware.**

When people start this practice, they may feel discomfort in the body. Certain muscles, like the abdominals, are required to keep the back straight. If you don't use these muscles regularly they may ache a little to begin with. This is normal. Many of us spend hours each day slouching on chairs; and during that time those muscles aren't being used. After a while and with practice, discomfort passes as the muscles strengthen. That's another advantage of having a straight posture – more physical strength. People look beautiful when they have a good posture. This is because you're observing a physical indication of free-flowing energy and awareness.

Being in pain is unpleasant. There's no denying that. However, what's great about experiencing pain is that you can use it as an opportunity to cultivate awareness. This goes for physical and emotional pain. That said, you should still do things to alleviate pain. For example, if you have a headache, you might want to take a couple of tablets to reduce the discomfort. If you're regularly experiencing emotional pain and feel overwhelmed, it's worth considering raising the issue with your doctor or getting some help from a therapist. Over the years, many of my friends and I have used therapy for all sorts of problems. As a result of this, I've learned lots about how my mind works. I've broken free of a great deal of suffering caused by repetitive unhelpful thought patterns and emotions. Sometimes it's right to raise the white flag and request support.

Mindfulness has been actively used to manage physical pain for years. If you're aware of physical sensations of pain, rather than being lost in your emotions or thoughts about them, you transcend the pain. You become the awareness rather than the pain. It doesn't necessarily stop the pain, but it does provide perspective on it, and enables you to be at peace. Gaining perspective on physical pain in this way allows you to view pain as a natural part of The Process. Physical pain is often exacerbated through getting lost in negative thinking. Being aware of pain prevents this and may even help to remove the pain altogether.

> 〞 **The next time you're experiencing unpleasant emotions, if the conditions allow you to, bring full awareness to them. Focus on them fully. Allow yourself to feel the unpleasantness within your body. Accept the feelings, and create a positive opportunity to heal.**

The Yoga Sutras claim this is a way of purifying yourself of karma; a way of burning up impressions stored within you, created by unskillful deeds, either within this lifetime or previous lifetimes. Karma is very much related to The Guidelines. Negative karma is created, and stored within you, when you're misaligned. Positive karma is created and stored within you when you're aligned. Another good reason to practice.

You enjoy increased confidence through this practice of healing emotional pain. It's about learning to accept emotional pain, and building faith that you can deal with anything that's presented to you. It's never people or situations that we're afraid of. We're afraid of not being able to accept our own feelings – that's what causes the fear. Accepting emotional pain may be used as a dedicated area of practice. I've had many times in my life where I've had to work diligently with this, and lighten other areas of practice for a while. We experience spells of emotional pain, like experiencing spells of weather – it comes and goes.

I would like to point out in this section that I'm not in any way condoning the *creation* of physical or emotional pain to provide stimulus for your practice. This would disregard the guideline on kindness, leading to psychological and possibly physical suffering. Life presents us with just enough physical and emotional pain for our practice. The Process intelligently balances out pain across the billions of people on the planet. It's quite impressive how it does that. Practice awareness and be grateful for the pain you do experience, as it represents an opportunity to heal and progress. Have faith that The Process will create just enough pain for you and everybody else based upon what's required for the whole to evolve. You grow through pain, and when your pain is active, you should use it as an opportunity for awareness and acceptance. Don't go creating anymore pain for yourself!

Finally, to help us become more aware, we can change our conditions so that we become less intoxicated, and gain more control over our minds. Intoxication bursts us outside of our field of awareness. We lose our connection with the intelligence from The Process, and the ego takes over. There's a temporary reduction or loss of control, of our thoughts, communication, and physical actions. This then leads to unskillful action, and misalignment. Intoxication isn't just caused by things like alcohol, caffeine and other drugs. You can intoxicate your mind with all sorts of things including sex, power, fantasy, compliments, exercise, and cravings.

> **Identify your own triggers for intoxication, then take steps to ensure you reduce the likelihood of becoming intoxicated. Either take yourself away from the triggers or increase the intensity of your awareness when you know you're at risk.**

Intoxication is often disguised as a positive thing. I've experienced this myself with caffeine. Also, with endorphins during excessive exercise. My mind runs away with itself, in a stream of uncontrollable thoughts that are all pointing towards experiencing pleasure, or achieving this or that. I used to fantasize about being famous and loved by millions of people! It was my ego's way of making up for a lack of self-esteem. The exciting feelings I'd experience when this happened were pleasurable, but they were created through a dream in my mind. Once I come down from the intoxicating thoughts, I felt sad or depressed as my mind regulated itself to bring me back to reality. Intoxication disguises itself positively or negatively.

> **Allow your true awareness to become an intoxication detective. Spot the times when your mind is becoming, or has been intoxicated – then reflect on what needs to change to help you stay more aware and grounded in the future.**

Patience with practice

Your current level of awareness is the awareness you were born with, plus any increase or decrease caused by your life conditions over the years. Some children are far more aware and conscious than their siblings, despite having the same parents and upbringing. Although, I cannot scientifically prove it, I believe this is evidence of rebirth. Every new child inherits a level of awareness from their previous lives. When you look at things in this way you can see that we are all processes of evolution spanning many lifetimes. These processes, or people as we call ourselves, are all connected, and a part of The Process.

Over the years, I've needed to work hard at becoming more aware. During earlier parts of my life, I was continuously lost in my thoughts and emotions. Most of the time I was anxious, with little self-awareness. Lack of awareness goes hand in hand with unskillfulness. My lack of awareness and inflated ego caused suffering for myself and others. As a child, I used to steal, communicate violently and act violently. On a couple of occasions, I was even prosecuted for my wrongdoings. Being locked up in a police cell didn't wake me up! It was through spiritual teachings, diligent practice, and changing my life conditions, that I was able to turn things around. It's taken many years to get to the point where I feel relatively mindful and skillful. I still get lost in thought and act unskillful occasionally, but it's subtle and infrequent compared to before.

The reason I'm telling you all of this, is to highlight that becoming more aware is usually a multi-year task. For most of us, progress is steady. Patience is required. The good news is that we see the fruits of our practice along the way. It's not as though we have to meditate every day for five years before anything positive happens. Through undertaking mindfulness and meditation practices, you literally transform your mind, speech and actions. Over the course of a few weeks or months, you observe that your mind is more peaceful. You notice your life becoming more harmonious.

In many ways, I'm grateful for my difficult conditions earlier in life. I've had to work hard at understanding and practicing the guidelines you find in this book. Most of the time, that process has been independent of religion or guidance from others. There are lots of people out there who have far greater awareness than I have, but they wouldn't know where to start in explaining how to cultivate it. This is similar to people who have been born into wealthy families and who haven't needed to earn their own money. They may have plenty of money, but have little knowledge or experience in earning it.

As with anything, if you're starting from what you believe is a difficult position, feeling like you've got a mountain to climb, then celebrate! You'll enjoy learning lots and making a great deal of progress. Many people that progress in this way become good advocates and guides, as they develop a deep understanding of the teachings.

Awareness during sleep

As your practice of this guideline advances you'll experience more awareness and stillness during sleep. When we sleep we're either in a dream state, or a dreamless state. The dream state is analogous to being lost in thought. It's a more intense version of what happens when your mind drifts off during the day whilst your eyes are open. The dreamless state is active when your mind is quiet and still. The body matches this and remains largely still during these times. It's at this time when you establish a deep connection to the intelligence within The Process. The intermediate state between these two types of sleep is when you bring awareness to your dreams, commonly known as lucid dreaming. This is analogous to observing your experience during the day through mindfulness practice. As you practice this guideline your ability to dream lucidly will be enhanced.

The more dreamless sleep you experience the better. You can prove this for yourself by using a device to monitor your sleep. Many sleep monitors and apps call dreamless sleep 'deep sleep,' That's a good name for it as during those times your mind is integrating more deeply into The Process's intelligence. Most devices track deep sleep by monitoring physical stillness. What you find, generally speaking, is that the deeper your sleep, the more wellness, peace and positivity you experience the following day. The reverse of this is true. When you spend most of the night restlessly dreaming, you feel tired and unpleasant the following day.

> **If you're at a stage where you can be present on demand, then it's worth reminding yourself to become present just before sleep.**

If this isn't possible for you, then observe the breath, or practice body awareness. These techniques increase your chances of being more present during sleep, which will lead to greater alignment, and increased wellness.

As your level of consciousness increases, you'll have the opportunity to apply The Guidelines in your dreams. This is an advanced faculty. The dreams your mind creates and how you conduct yourself within dreams, create mental impressions and emotions. These impressions then inform your future interactions within The Process. Feeling unpleasant after a bad dream, and then allowing that feeling to trigger unkind behavior towards others is an example of this. A positive example is being kind to somebody you don't usually like whilst dreaming, and then feeling compelled to be kind to them the following day. Your responses to the content of dreams can help or hinder your alignment. Although it feels like you're creating your dreams, it's actually The Process that's the source of creation. And your mind is the platform simulating the dream experience. It's analogous to your mind being like a TV whilst The Process is transmitting the signal to control the content. Who you think you are is the central actor in the TV show.

Your awareness and conduct within every sleeping experience falls into one of the four categories below. They're listed in order of consciousness, from least conscious to most conscious.

1. Upon waking, you cannot recall dreams, and you're unaware whilst dreaming.
2. Upon waking, you can recall dreams. During dreams, you're unaware that you're dreaming. The experience feels the same as your waking life.
3. You're aware of dreams and can recall them. You know you're dreaming whilst you dream (lucid dreaming). However, you're not practicing The Guidelines whilst dreaming.
4. In addition to recalling dreams and lucid dreaming, you practice The Guidelines within dreams; including your thoughts, communication and physical actions.

Here is a tabularized version of the four levels of consciousness:

Level of consciousness	Recalling dreams	Lucid dreaming	Practicing The Guidelines whilst dreaming
1	No	No	No
2	Yes	No	No
3	Yes	Yes	No
4	Yes	Yes	Yes

Your dreams are a good measure of progress with this guideline. If you start recollecting dreams more, knowing when you're dreaming, and consciously following The Guidelines within dreams, you're making progress and on the right track.

Connections with other guidelines

All seven guidelines connect together, and support each other. The table below highlights a few of the connections between, "Be present, bringing awareness and acceptance into every moment" and the other guidelines:

Guideline	Connections
Honor the body	• Accepting the body including condition, shape, bodily sensations, feelings and general health. • Awareness of the energy within the body. • Awareness of bodily sensations and feelings. • Awareness of the position and posture of the body. • Awareness of the needs of the body. • Awareness of pleasure, discomfort and pain within the body. • Awareness just prior to sleep, and during sleep. • Bringing awareness and acceptance to every moment leads to a peaceful mind. This naturally balances the energy in the body and conserves energy. • Negative emotions deplete energy within the body. Accepting them helps them to pass, and conserves energy.
Act with kindness, considering everyone and everything	• Bring a kindly acceptance to physical and emotional pain, whilst taking practical steps to avoid their triggers. • True kindness is only accessible through the present moment. • Practicing acceptance is a form of kindness.
Understand the truth, communicating it selectively and skillfully	• The truth can only be understood through the present moment. Not when you're lost in thought. • The truth can only be communicated selectively and skillfully in the present moment. Not when you're lost in thought. • If it's possible and appropriate, get to the truth of situations to help yourself with relative acceptance.
Do only what needs to be done	• The infinite intelligence within The Process can only guide your actions based on its needs, when you're aware and accepting your experience in the present moment. • Being present is a joy in itself. • As you become more present, your ego will have less desire to do things. • If you do less, you may find yourself with more opportunities to heal emotional pain.
Harmoniously obtain and retain only what you need	• Ultimately, to be present is the only thing to obtain and retain. • Through being present, you'll have a lightness in relation to wanting things from the world.
Apply The Guidelines to your digital device usage	• Bring awareness and acceptance to your experience with digital devices. • Let go of accessing digital content that triggers states of resistance.

You can find a list of ideas for practicing this guideline in the final chapter "Building & Structuring Your Practice."

POINTS FOR REFLECTION

1. Mindfulness is awareness and acceptance of bodily sensations, feelings and thoughts, within the present moment.

2. When you're mindful whilst being receptive to the intelligence within The Process, you practice more than just standard mindfulness. This is Mindfulness+.

3. The only way you can be in alignment with what's happened, and what's to come, is through the present moment.

4. It can be helpful to ask yourself, "Am I present?" When you ask yourself this question, you automatically become present.

5. Bringing awareness to something real like the energy in your hands, or another part of the body, is a good way of regaining and sustaining presence.

6. When you observe unpleasant feelings without distracting yourself, some or all of the pain associated with them is released. This is the process of healing.

7. For most of us, our increase in mindfulness will be gradual, and may be accelerated through spiritual practice.

8. Setting up a regular meditation practice will most certainly improve your awareness.

9. Maintaining awareness on your breath will keep you grounded, whatever activity you're involved in.

10. Components of our Experience: Thoughts, Feelings & Bodily Sensations.

11. The Two Modes of the Mind:
    – "Lost" in thought
    – Being present/Mindfulness+.

12. The Four A's: <u>A</u>wareness ▸ <u>A</u>cceptance ▸ <u>A</u>ligned <u>A</u>ction.

Act with Kindness, Considering Everyone and Everything

Stated negatively: Do not be intentionally harmful or single-minded in your actions

KINDNESS TOWARDS PEOPLE means being considerate, friendly and generous. The vision is that all your actions consider the whole. The Process is appreciative and rewarding when you take a wider view, rather than just considering yourself, another individual or group. The opposite to kindness is intentionally causing harm. The Process rewards us for deeds of kindness, and corrects us for deeds of harm. There are always consequences for our actions. This phenomenon is known as karma in many religions and philosophies.

Guideline: Act with Kindness

At other times they manifest externally through other people and forms. Sometimes the consequences only show themselves internally within us, through our thoughts and feelings. This is all due to the processes we influence through our actions. Action can be thought, communication, or physical action. The Process uses its infinite intelligence to decide which karmic consequences to manifest. The consequences will often be experienced in our current lifetime. Sometimes, consequences manifest later in time, after our physical body has died, and manifest within a future life. Every action is reconciled by The Process through reward or correction at some point or another.

I use the phrases '*deeds* of kindness' and '*deeds* of harm.' To perform a deed, there must be an intention. Rewards and corrections are linked to the intentions, not the fruits of your deeds. For example, if you were to give a homeless person a sandwich, and she threw it back at you complaining about the filling, you'd still be rewarded. In the same way, if you tried to hurt somebody by saying something unkind, but it had no impact on them, you'd still be corrected. Rewards take the form of pleasant experiences, whilst corrections take the form of suffering. It's impossible to achieve your desired results with every deed. The Process is too vast and complex for that. However, your intentions are fully within your control, so you can take responsibility for them. Hence the link between intention and consequence. It's fine for you to have a positive goal or intention, so long as you aren't attached to the outcome. The kindness guideline title reflects this, through use of the word *act* with kindness. It doesn't say achieve results or attach to results.

If you're kind to someone, and they return the kindness in some way, that's the result of a process you've initiated. The Process often arranges things in that way as a reward, even if you didn't want anything in return. Sometimes it arranges for you to be rewarded or corrected through people or situations that don't appear to be linked to the deed. Often, it's clear to see what previous action caused your correction or reward; and sometimes it's unclear. As I said before, the time taken for rewards or corrections to manifest is unknown. It can take anything from a millisecond to a few lifetimes. Sometimes, there doesn't seem to be any external rewards for kindness. Instead, you appear to experience pleasant feelings or positive thoughts during the action. The same can be said for actions with an intention to harm. There may appear to be no negative consequences other than unpleasant feelings or thoughts during the action. There will always be consequences in some shape or form, at some point.

I recall times when I've experienced serious psychological and emotional suffering as a result of being unkind and harmful in my communication and actions. As painful as they were at the time, these corrections helped me understand the unskillfulness of my deeds. People become aligned with The Guidelines through corrections, regardless of whether they understand the things I'm explaining in this book. If you resist the correction, rather than accept it, The Process will continue to apply corrections until you're corrected. The Process may increase the intensity of the correction, which leads to greater pain. This is why acceptance is so important.

> Ideally, we should accept initial corrections fully; learning from them, and freeing ourselves from pain in the future.

The best advice I can provide, is to stay very aware before, during and following your actions. The more you do this, the kinder you become. Your body always provides you with feedback in the form of pleasant and unpleasant feelings. The secret is to acknowledge the feedback through awareness and acceptance.

Sometimes, despite your best efforts, you feel unkind regardless of the course of action. People can experience this when they're in a dysfunctional relationship. It feels unkind to stay in the relationship, and unkind to leave it. You have to do one or the other. Whichever option you choose leads to suffering. This is part of human life. There will always be the potential for suffering where there are attachments. The suffering is created by The Process to bring attachments, and their consequences, to our attention. In these situations, it's always best to take the path of least harm. The path of least harm is the path of kindness.

The source of kindness

When you observe the world in operation, you'll see that kindness flows abundantly. Kindness even flows at a universal level. The sun has been kind to life forms on the earth for millions of years. Kindness is sourced from the infinite intelligence within The Process. It's for this reason that kindness is also infinite. If you asked me, "What is the source of anything?" I could give you the same answer: The infinite intelligence within The Process. I cannot explain this to you adequately in words because what I'm pointing to is formless. Words are things; they are form-based. You cannot explain something formless with form. This intelligence I refer to, also known as wisdom, is something you connect with naturally by following The Guidelines and understanding The Process.

The Selfishness/Altruism Intention Scale

Our intentions always fall somewhere on the Selfishness / Altruism Intention Scale as shown below:

The Selfishness/Altruism Intention Scale

At one end of the scale are totally selfish deeds. Things that you do purely for yourself, without any consideration for others. At the other end of the scale are totally altruistic deeds. These are kind deeds, with no expectations for yourself. It's difficult to say whether deeds can really be at either extreme on the scale. The question over whether totally altruistic deeds are possible has been debated for years. If we understand The Process, we know we'll always be rewarded at some point for our good deeds.

What I can say for sure, is the greater your alignment, the more likely it is that you'll act altruistically. When you're aligned, you make decisions based on what's right for the whole. This happens when you're being present, bringing awareness and acceptance into every moment. Even on a local scale, you need to be present to be kind. You need to stay aware to notice that somebody might be upset, and ask if they're OK. Awareness is essential. And kindness flows out of a state of acceptance. If you're resisting the present moment, your action will be harmful.

Applying the guideline

It can be easy to misread this guideline believing you must do things like giving all of your money to charity, leaving your partner so they can be free to meet somebody who will be better for them than you, doing altruistic work and so on. It may be that people will need to do some or all of these things, and that's fine. Regardless of what you do, your current life situation is a platform for kindness. It doesn't matter who you are, where you are, what you're doing, and with whom. There are always opportunities for practicing kindness and the other guidelines.

Speaking to people in call centers is a golden opportunity to be kind. We should remember that the person on the other end of the phone is a human being with feelings. I recall a guy ringing me up once, trying to sell me something. He said, "Hello, how are you?" I said, "I'm doing good, how are things with you?" I was genuinely interested in how he was. He said I was the first person that day to ask him how he was doing. He really appreciated it. If I'm being honest with you, I've also been unkind to people in call centers when I've been frustrated and angry. That doesn't feel good. It's much better all round when people are considerate towards each other. It creates positive energy. It doesn't take long. You don't need to stay on calls longer than is necessary. You can be kind quickly.

Hanging out with kind people, and spending time in kind environments, helps you become kinder. The opposite is also true – if you hang out with unkind people, or base yourself in unkind environments, this will increase your chances of being unkind. These are general rules. Common sense tells you there will be exceptions. For example, you may be performing a kind role in an unkind environment. The scenario of a kind doctor called out to treat an injured worker in a slaughterhouse would fit within this category.

There are always opportunities to be kind to yourself, and more often than not, opportunities to be kind to others, and things external to you. Simple things like smiling and saying thank you are wonderful. I asked friends about significant acts of kindness they'd experienced and observed. Funnily enough, it was the small and simple things they mentioned. One example included a work colleague always smiling and saying hello when she walked into the office. Another example was a friend who rescued an injured sparrow on the road. A man had to stop his van to allow her to move the bird into the hedgerow. He observed what she did and stepped out of his van. He then told her that was the kindest act he'd seen in a long time, and gave her a hug! I'm guessing he then spread that kindness in other ways throughout the day. One of the magical things about kindness is that it propagates. A small act of kindness is like dropping a pebble into a still lake. It ripples out in all directions.

You can also be kind to things, like plants and objects. I feel kind when I'm watering my plants. When I'm cleaning my bathroom and making it look tidy and sparkling, it feels like I'm being kind to the bathroom. I feel like I'm expressing my thanks and gratitude towards things when I clean or maintain them. Cleaning is a great mindfulness practice.

"" Try mindful cleaning. Give the whole experience your full attention. It can be a very pleasurable thing to do.

The three components of kindness (consideration, friendliness and generosity) may be expressed through thoughts, communication, or physical acts. Each of these different channels for kindness are equally powerful, and will create a ripple effect out into the world. Given how connected we all are through the Internet, kindness can spread thousands of miles without us even leaving our homes or speaking to people. Kindness also spreads through a subtler channel that we cannot yet comprehend. Interestingly, the channels for kindness interact, and promote each other. For example, kind thoughts often lead to kind communication, and physical acts. The reverse is true. Kind communication and physical acts will often lead to kind thoughts. I was definitely kinder whilst writing this chapter. Even writing or reading about kindness is an act of kindness in itself, because it cultivates kindness.

When your ego's active, the source of kindness is temporarily blocked. The ego is like a valve in a water tap, preventing the water from running freely. Even when the tap is switched off, the pressure is still there. Although it's not visible, the water is longing to be released during these times. The water in this analogy represents kindness. We experience unpleasant feelings when the ego's active. Feelings like irrational forms of anger, jealousy and anxiety. These, and all the other unpleasant feelings we experience, prevent us from being kind. Sometimes, the unpleasant feelings are needed to trigger change and alignment. They're gifts from The Process. By bringing awareness and acceptance to these feelings, we allow The Process to heal and guide us.

We're all works in progress, and sometimes we resist our feelings, no matter how hard we try to be present.

"" When you experience repeatable themes of resistance, preventing you from being peaceful and kind, consider investigating them.

You might choose to get help from friends, or support from a therapist. It can be beneficial to do some reflection and analytical thinking, to help you get closer to the truth of what's going on. This will place your mind in a stronger position to accept the situation. Use relative acceptance through analysis of the situation; and absolute acceptance of the specific feelings as they arise.

The root causes for irrational unpleasant emotions will always be old pain that you have stored within your body. A substantial part of practicing kindness is taking responsibility to heal this pain through awareness and acceptance.

Being considerate

The first component of kindness is being considerate. Being considerate is about considering the feelings of yourself and others. It's also about being considerate towards everything else; all of nature. This aligns with the guideline: Act with kindness, considering everyone and everything. Consideration follows the model:

<u>A</u>wareness ▶ <u>A</u>cceptance ▶ <u>A</u>ligned <u>A</u>ction

Apart from in emergency situations, consideration of yourself should always come first. The justification for this, is that if you're aware of your experience, and managing your own feelings, you'll be in a stronger position to consider others. A good analogy is applying your own oxygen mask on a plane before you help others apply theirs. If you're resisting feelings, due to a lack of awareness or for some other reason, your action will be misaligned. Do you recall the two modes of the mind from Chapter Four? Kindness flows out of being present. I've included the illustrations of the two models below to act as a reminder.

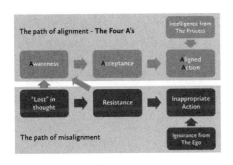

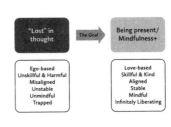

The Four A's   The Two Modes of the Mind

Consideration flows through the path of alignment when we're being present. The same goes for the other forms of kindness I'll introduce shortly. In fact, any form of skillfulness or aligned action follows this same path. A few examples of consideration are:

- Identifying and meeting the need for some time alone.
- Recognizing a friend is looking unwell, and sensitively inquiring into how they're feeling.
- Giving plants water when they need it.
- Considering our neighbors when we're making noise at home.
- Letting go of acquiring products you know are sourced unethically.
- Turning up to meet a friend at the time you agreed.
- Bringing awareness to one of your addictions, and taking responsibility to reduce or remove it.
- Removing an insect carefully from your home rather than killing it.

The reason I've shared these examples is to demonstrate the wide scope of consideration. Awareness enables consideration. It means we can be receptive to the needs of ourselves, other people, and other things. We don't have the capacity to be aware of every need. Similarly, we may not be able to respond to every need we're aware of – so we have to prioritize.

Consideration is a matter of priority. Sometimes, priorities are obvious. If somebody close by has been involved in a fatal accident, you go to help if it's safe to do so, or you call for help. You don't waste time reflecting on whether the flowers nearby have had enough rain, or if there's something else more important to do. That's an obvious example. How do we prioritize subtler opportunities for consideration? I've asked myself that a number of times. I'll be sat at my computer writing, then stop what I'm doing and question whether I should be doing that, or something else more important. The answer is usually that I should be writing the book, because if I was aware of something more important to do, I'd be doing it. As a general rule, if you're not confident anything else needs your attention more than what you're doing now, then you should continue with it. This links in with the Guideline "Do only what needs to be done," which I'll be detailing in Chapter Seven.

Consideration is essential when you're communicating. This is linked with the guideline, "Understand the truth, communicating it selectively and skillfully," which I'll be detailing in the following chapter. Truthful, selective, and skilful communication, must be preceded by consideration. If a sensitive friend invites you to dinner and you didn't enjoy the food you were served, it would usually be kinder to keep your opinion to yourself, rather than to disclose it there and then.

> 🙶 **Sometimes, it's right to share something that you believe somebody is going to find difficult to hear. In these cases, you do so sensitively.**

Select an appropriate time, place, and way of communicating. This is all part of being kind.

It's quite normal to expect things from yourself and others. You need expectations to function in the world. Openness and faith to what may be, should wrap around goals and expectations. Identification with an expectation leads to misalignment and suffering. Let's say you're planning to take an exam. Expecting to pass it is fine. Identifying with passing it, and believing it's guaranteed, will cause stress. You'll either suffer if you fail; be anxious whilst waiting for the result; or experience an intoxicating high, complacency, or attachment to what you've gained if you pass. When we have expectations without being identified with them, we remain peaceful and balanced, regardless of the outcome. We can enjoy success without getting lost in it. Allowing what is, being free from identification with expectations in relation to ourselves or others, makes us kinder and more accepting. You may have experienced this for yourself. When people are peaceful and kind to you, regardless of what you do, it feels pleasant and helpful. When people express feelings of anger, aversion, and resistance towards you, it can feel unpleasant and unhelpful.

Finally, on the subject of being considerate, I'd like to point out that every act of kindness is also an act of consideration. Consideration is a synonym for kindness.

Being friendly

Being kind means being friendly. If you think about times when people have been friendly to you, what did they all have in common? Interest. To be friendly to somebody, you must be interested in them. It's the interest in somebody that provides you with energy to act. Friendliness is an active quality. I've broken down the process of friendliness in a diagram to help explore what's happening. I call this process *The Steps to Friendliness*.

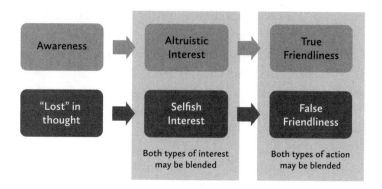

The Steps to Friendliness

As with many other practices, this starts with awareness. You notice more awareness in people who are friendly. They're tuned in to what's going on around them. In particular, what's going on with other people. Their interest in themselves and others is balanced optimally for what's needed at the time. When people are lost in their thoughts or emotions, they're unable to tune into what's happening around them, making it impossible for them to be truly friendly.

False friendliness occurs when somebody is friendly with mainly selfish intentions. Disinterest in others occurs through overly emphasizing oneself. In these cases, the person is unable to be kind to others, as they're following a process in their own minds with them at the center of the universe. Their ego has taken over. People do this for all sorts of genuine reasons. Over the years, I've been regularly disinterested in others whilst socializing. It's not because I'm a bad man. It's just that my past conditioning, particularly during childhood, caused me to be afraid and self-conscious. People's ability to be friendly can be dependent upon what's going on for them at the time. If they're less present because of some inner excitement or stress for example, like in my case, their awareness and therefore their friendliness, will be lower.

To cultivate friendliness, we need to cultivate awareness of others. This includes when we're with people physically, on the telephone, or connecting via digital means. It also means being aware of others when they're not around. When we're present, the mind has an impressive way of being able to tune into everybody, and how they're feeling. It does this by utilizing subtle channels within The Process that connect us all. Through this awareness we're able to mentally inquire into how people are and what they need. For example, we may ask ourselves how a friend is doing who we know is attending a hospital appointment. Or we may just randomly feel an urge to connect with somebody who needs our contact, even although we don't know why. The intelligence within The Process is able to prioritize our interest in others through our awareness, without us consciously thinking about it.

The second stage in The Steps to Friendliness is interest. After becoming aware, there must be some interest in another person to create the energy for us to take friendly action. The friendly action may be anything from smiling briefly at a stranger, to organizing a party for a friend you've known since childhood. Where does this interest in others come from? Interest that leads to pure friendliness always comes from a place of love and altruism. In reality, interest for most people, usually contains a blend of both selfish and altruistic motives. It sits on the Selfishness / Altruism Intention Scale introduced earlier.

Because most interest contains selfish and altruistic motives, actions are typically a blend of both true friendliness and false friendliness, as shown in The Steps to Friendliness model. I experience this when I'm promoting books. When I engage with potential readers there are usually three things going on. Firstly, I'm genuinely interested in them as a person. Secondly, I'm genuinely wanting to help them through the teachings in my book. And thirdly, being honest, my ego is wanting praise and positive feedback on how great my writing is, and how spiritual I am! The selfish interest always comes from things that our egos identify with. All three motives provide me with the energy to be friendly whilst promoting books.

Compliments are a form of friendliness. To pay somebody a *real compliment* requires awareness, interest, altruism, and alignment. A real compliment is when you compliment somebody on being aligned, without any selfish interest, or attachment to the potential results. I'm not suggesting you say, "Wow – what you just did was really aligned with guideline number three." No, that would be dull! Complimenting somebody on when they've been kind, told the truth, communicated skillfully, honored their body, and so on, is the way to go. That acknowledges their alignment and your appreciation of The Guidelines.

Having selfish components to our friendliness is natural. It's fine to be friendly when there's an element of selfishness. It's only when the selfishness is harmful in some way or dominates the intention that we should review letting go of our 'friendly' actions. In the book example, if I were mainly interested in praise and positive feedback, with little consideration for potential readers, then it would be unskillful for me to engage with them.

Even if I did, most of them wouldn't be interested as they'd sense selfishness in the communication.

Friendliness isn't just about others. It's also about being friendly to yourself. I discussed this in the guideline, "Honor the Body." Giving your body what it needs is a genuine type of friendliness. The mind needs friendliness too. Through awareness, we can spot when we need to help ourselves psychologically through activities such as resolving inner conflicts, and relaxing our busy minds. If you're unfriendly to your body and mind, you'll find yourself in a state of resistance with little opportunity for awareness of others. True friendliness towards others is only possible from a platform of friendliness to yourself. Being friendly to yourself in a positive way like this is never selfish. With the right intention, it's altruistic. You wish to be friendly to yourself because you're honoring The Process that created you, and have a need to keep yourself in good condition for the service of others.

The scope of friendliness is far greater than yourself and other people. This is why I called this guideline, "Act with kindness, considering everyone and *everything*." We can be friendly to a fence by painting it; or a dog by patting it. Keeping your living environment clean and tidy is an example of friendliness towards the living environment. Have you noticed how good it feels to look at an environment that's been cleaned with love? It's as though the place is smiling at you. The environment is expressing its gratitude. Shutting doors carefully and mindfully rather than slamming them is also a form of friendliness. You can be friendly to a charitable organization by donating time or money. Don't get too caught up with trying to think about what or whom you should be friendly towards. There are too many opportunities to analyze with conscious thought.

> Stay relaxed, alert and aware. Allow The Process to inform you where you need to channel your kindness.

I recall many times in my life when I've been friendly to people because I was sad and lonely. I'd use people selfishly for my own pleasure or some other gain. My ego had little interest in them as a person. As you can imagine, this type of friendliness doesn't really work, and usually leads to more suffering for yourself, and others. It's the kind of friendliness that feels odd when you're on the receiving end. It has a strange energy to it that causes you to want to move away from the person being 'friendly.'

You have to watch out for instances like this where the selfish component of interest dominates. As I said earlier, there's often some selfishness motivating friendliness. However, when it's the lion share of motivation, we need to do some work to take responsibility for whatever personal dysfunction is driving it.

> Be careful about embracing friendliness from others
> if you suspect their motives are mainly selfish as it will
> lead to suffering.

Finally, I'd like to point out that every act of kindness is also an act of friendliness. Friendliness is a synonym for kindness.

Being generous

The Process appreciates kindness in the form of generosity. This creative and positive flow of energy is an acknowledgement of your understanding that you're connected to everybody and everything else. You are part of something infinite. This is why *true generosity* feels so good and yields favorable results. This happens every time you give without expecting anything in return. The opposite to this is *false generosity*, which is when you give solely because you expect something in return from whom you are giving. The Selfishness / Altruism Intention Scale applies here, and like other forms of kindness, our motives for being generous are often mixed. True generosity builds relationships. It removes the focus from your false sense of self, reducing your attachments. It feels good, diminishes the ego, and reduces greed. When you're generous to people you don't like, which for some people includes themselves, it reduces hatred and cultivates love. Feelings of depression and isolation can be reduced; and replaced with contentment and connectedness. Every generous action progresses you spiritually. Whichever way you look at it, practicing generosity makes sense.

Generosity is expressed in many ways. For example, you can give time, money, physical energy, material things or knowledge. Helping people in a positive way is a form of generosity. Taking steps to keep yourself and others safe is an example of this. You can be generous in your behaviors by providing others with confidence and positivity.

> Simply being present in somebody's company and listening to
> them is a generous act.

Many people are generous in their work through doing a helpful job and kindly serving others. Some highly generous people will even give their own lives for the sake of others.

You can be generous to yourself, a single person, a group of people, another living being like an animal, and even things that are insentient. Planting seeds is being generous to the tree or plant that produced them. It's generous to receive from others who are giving with wholesome motives, as you're enabling them to execute a good deed.

> Receiving from insentient sources is a form of generosity. By receiving from nature, you're giving it the opportunity to be appreciated and express its gratitude for being there.

True generosity is a special form of energy that whilst flowing, enables people to let go of their sense of separateness. You can view everybody with equal regard; even your 'enemies.' Every positive opportunity to give is a gift; another opportunity to become more aligned.

The opposite to being generous is stealing. Taking things without the permission of those who own it. Examples of things you give apply to things you steal. When we talk about stealing, we often think about material things. Stealing is much more than this. You can steal by taking somebody's time if they're not freely giving it. Intruding is a form of stealing. Also, if you're harming your own body, you're stealing its health. When you stop and contemplate this you'll soon realize that stealing has a very broad scope. Part of the practice of being generous is also to practice non-stealing.

Generousness and non-stealing call for awareness and presence. True generosity always stems from kindness. If you're considered in your giving, what you give is far more likely to have a positive impact on the recipients. We receive feedback from The Process through our experience of feelings in the body. After you've been generous, you can determine where the generous act lies on the Selfishness / Altruism Intention Scale, and how considered you were. Pleasant feelings signify alignment, whilst unpleasant feelings signify misalignment. The Process may also provide feedback through others in the form of their positive responses, or negative reactions.

Let's contemplate feedback from others. It's easy to believe that praise from others is a sign of alignment; and that disapproval from others is a sign of misalignment. That's not always the case. Especially if those giving the feedback are lost in thought, or emotional, whilst they communicate. You can be praised for doing something unskillful, and disapproved of for doing something skillful. This type of communication stems from somebody's ego rather than who they truly are.

> **When you receive feedback from others, in whatever form it takes, be very present.**

When you're present, you'll be able to validate for yourself whether the giver of the feedback is communicating truthfully. If they are, always express your gratitude – regardless of whether it feels pleasant or unpleasant. If their feedback is false, then discard it, let it go. Observe yourself carefully to ensure that your ego doesn't use it as fuel. It can be all too easy to get caught up in other people's opinions about you. Stay present, stay grounded.

I've struggled with giving money and material things over the years. I used to be so stingy! I recall going to the bar with friends when I was younger. I'd become anxious when it was time for somebody to pay for the drinks. The thought of buying a round and not getting back the financial equivalent of what I'd purchased for others filled me with dread. It's quite common for those who view themselves as being separate, to keep count of things in this way. Even today, after working hard with my spiritual practice, I still have times when I find it hard to give – even to family and close friends. Sometimes, I can be outwardly generous, but when I give things away or purchase things for people, it can feel painful. This is because of past conditioning and pain triggered by my ego. There was definitely a scarcity mentality around when I was younger, which contributed to this dysfunction. The ego is afraid and greedy by nature, it wants to cling onto things it's identified with like possessions and wealth.

These days, I try and give as much as I can, even if I know it's difficult and might feel unpleasant. The unpleasantness I feel during the giving is old emotional reactions that have been programmed into my mind from a young age. Over time and with plenty of awareness, they've reduced. When I become aware of these feelings and let them go, I always feel positive about being generous. It's essential to become aware of your ego's shortcomings like this; to transcend them with spiritual confidence. You then do the right thing, and align yourself with The Guidelines, regardless of your past conditioning. You literally rise above your own ego and transcend to a wiser plane.

There's an important watch out when it comes to being generous. In parallel with giving to others, you also need to be kind to yourself. Giving too much, to the extent where you're incapable of meeting your own needs, is not real generosity. It's caused by a form of egoic-driven false generosity and ignorance towards your own needs. This type of action leads to resentment and suffering. It can apply to any type of generosity. It might be giving material things, or more subtle forms of generosity, like giving somebody your time and energy when your resources are depleted. It's a form of kindness, to take responsibility for yourself; ensuring your own needs are met.

There will be times when you do need to be generous, whilst accepting that there's an associated cost to you. For example, if a parent is tired, and doesn't have anybody to look after their small child, they'll still need to feed and entertain them. Another example is when there's a need to give your time to be in the company of somebody who triggers unpleasant feelings within you. On the one hand you're being generous and doing what needs to be done, whilst on the other hand, it feels like you're harming yourself. The Process is at a stage in its evolution where humans cause harm and suffer. Realistically speaking, this means that even when we're practicing The Guidelines, it's highly likely we'll still be causing harm, although the extent of this does reduce through practice. You may need to take a sick family member to the hospital in your car and kill a few flies that hit your windscreen.

> 〞 The practice is to cultivate enough awareness so that you can consciously decide on the path of *least* harm.

In the example of being in somebody's company whom you find difficult, you can minimize the time you spend with them, or allow time for your own preparation and recovery. By continuing to take the path of least harm, you build your capacity to navigate kindly through life.

If you're giving money to somebody begging, do so carefully and respectfully. Whilst driving, if you're beckoning somebody to let them out in front of you on the road, do so in a friendly way with a smile. Giving is not just about what you give, it's also about how you give.

Being generous is a way of honoring The Process. When you're generous and you give something, including your energy, you're acknowledging that everything's connected, and that energy needs to flow between people and things. Generosity is energy. Being prepared to give your own life for others, in extreme circumstances, is the pinnacle of this faith, although I'm not suggesting you need to do that to make progress! With an inflated ego, a selfish attitude, and no faith in The Process, it's impossible to be generous. The ego is afraid that if you give away too much, it will be unable to retain its identifications that it needs to exist. When you observe yourself becoming more generous, you can see it as a sign that your understanding and faith in The Process is growing, and your ego is diminishing. It's a good sign!

Finally, on the subject of being generous, I would like to point out that every act of kindness is also an act of generosity. Generosity is a synonym for kindness. In reality, kindness, consideration, friendliness and generosity are all one. Everything is one.

Six ways to cultivate kindness

Your capacity to be kind is dependent upon how The Process created you, your past conditioning, and your ability to be present. Whatever your level of kindness, the good news is that you can cultivate more of it. Deeds of kindness work well when they're spontaneous. When this happens, your actions come from a place of love and are likely to feel pleasant for the recipient. Another option is to sit down and consciously think about how to be kind to people, then plan activities to do so. This second approach is often led by the ego and can feel impure. It can also be used as a way of manipulating people. Mechanical kindness such as systematically liking friends' social media posts without really feeling a connection to them at the time is impure. You can't plan to be truly kind. However, you can plan to cultivate kindness.

I've worked hard at cultivating kindness over the years. It's not been a quick or easy process for me, and I still have much work to do. These days, I'm more often described as kind and I put that down to the work I've done to cultivate kindness through spiritual practice. There are six ways of cultivating kindness that have helped me over the years. I'd like to share them with you:

1 **Practice loving kindness meditation**

Also known as Metta Bhavana. This is a meditation practice that involves bringing to mind yourself, people to whom you can express kindness easily, people you have problems with, strangers, and then everybody else in the world. As you do this, you use your imagination to send them love and kindness. This meditation trains the subconscious mind to create kind thoughts, which in turn leads to spontaneous acts of kindness outside of meditation. Having tried it for years, and met many other people who have done the same, I can categorically state that this meditation practice can be highly effective. There are plenty of good books, courses, apps and guided walkthroughs that describe this meditation. Reading books from Sharon Salzberg[10] is a good place to start – Sharon is an internationally recognized expert in this area.

2 Do only what needs to be done

By following this guideline, which is detailed in Chapter Seven, we end up needing to do less for ourselves. We let go of spending time doing stuff that's unhelpful. The time that's freed up can then be used for the kind service of others. As I'm sure you'll appreciate, when you're too busy, it's virtually impossible to bring awareness or consideration to other people or things.

3 Be around kind people

Kindness is propagated by people. Everything else being equal, if you're around people who are generally kinder than yourself, you'll cultivate more kindness. To cultivate kindness, it helps if your close friends are kind. And groups that you socialize with, generally speaking, should be kind. This may include people at your place of work, and social groups you engage with.

4 Practice The Guidelines

Every guideline cultivates kindness and provides opportunities for kind deeds. I've included notes at the end of the chapter that highlight the connections between kindness and the other guidelines.

5 Embrace opportunities to be kind

There will be many times when acts of kindness enter your consciousness. It may be giving some food to a beggar, or randomly texting a friend to wish them well. If you're present, you'll know instantly whether these opportunities should be acted upon; and most of the time they should.

6 Accept kindness from others

Kindness from others comes in many forms. When you accept kindness, you're being generous. It's generous to the person who is being kind, plus you're acknowledging that they're following The Guidelines. It's also generous to yourself if their kindness is meeting a need of yours. This is the case when a friend listens patiently when you need to talk. It can be difficult to accept kindness sometimes. Especially if your ego views accepting kindness as a form of weakness; or if your ego feels threatened in some way. Accepting kindness from people you don't like can also be a challenge. When you accept kindness under difficult circumstances like these, it's a golden opportunity to deflate your ego and heal difficult relationships. Acceptance of kindness is acceptance of the love that connects us all.

Connections with other guidelines

All seven guidelines connect together, and support each other. The table below highlights a few of the connections between "Act with kindness, considering everyone and everything" and the other guidelines.

Guidelines	Connections
Honor the body	• Show the body friendliness, through awareness and interest. • Be generous to the body by caring for it, and giving it what it needs.
Be present, bringing awareness and acceptance into every moment	• True kindness is only accessible through the present moment. • Awareness is required to allow us to consider others, before we act kindly. • Through being present, you can access the infinite intelligence from The Process. This will prioritize where to invest energy used for kind acts. • With awareness, you identify when you need to help yourself, through activities such as resolving inner conflicts, and relaxing your mind. • When you're present, you're offered more opportunities to be kind.
Understand the truth, communicating it selectively and skillfully	• Consideration and kindness are essential when you're deciding what, where, when, and how to communicate. • Sometimes, it's right to share something you believe somebody is going to find difficult. In these cases, you do so sensitively.
Do only what needs to be done	• We let go of spending time doing stuff that isn't helpful or aligned. That time can then be used for the kind service of others. • When you're excessively busy, it's difficult to bring awareness or consideration to other people or things. • Real kindness is a form of karma yoga, as you're not attached to the results of your actions.

Guidelines	Connections
Harmoniously obtain and retain only what you need	• The fewer things you own, the fewer things you need to consider. Surplus energy and resources can be used for the kind service of others. • If you lead a simple life with only the items you need, you can be generous with surplus money or items. • It's a form of kindness to take responsibility for yourself; ensuring you obtain and retain what you need.
Apply The Guidelines to your digital device usage	• Digital channels are a medium for kindness. Apply this thought to your digital interactions with others.

You can find a list of ideas for practicing this guideline in the final chapter "Building & Structuring Your Practice."

POINTS FOR REFLECTION

1. The three components of kindness are consideration, friendliness and generosity.
2. Kindness flows out of acceptance.
3. Kindness is sourced from the infinite intelligence within The Process. It's for this reason that kindness is also infinite.
4. Spending time with kind people and being in kind environments, helps you cultivate kindness.
5. Simply being present in somebody's company, and listening to them, is a generous act.
6. You can't plan to be truly kind. It happens spontaneously. However, you can plan to cultivate kindness.
7. Acceptance of kindness from others is acceptance of the love that connects us all.
8. Every action is reconciled by The Process through reward or correction. These are linked to intentions, not the fruits of your deeds.
9. The Process rewards for deeds of kindness, and corrects for deeds of harm.
10. Six ways of cultivating kindness:
    a. Practice loving kindness meditation.
    b. Do only what needs to be done.
    c. Be around kind people.
    d. Practice The Guidelines.
    e. Embrace opportunities to be kind.
    f. Accept kindness from others.

Understand the Truth, Communicating It Selectively and Skillfully

Stated negatively: Avoid excessive, harmful and false communication

The Process enjoys being acknowledged accurately. It rewards people that understand and communicate the truth; and corrects those who do not. As with many characteristics of The Process, I cannot explain to you *why* this is the case. It just is. You can prove it by reflecting on your own experience. When you understand the truth, when you see clearly, you're at peace; regardless of whether it feels pleasant or unpleasant.

Guideline: Understand the Truth

The real truth will always bring about a peaceful acceptance of thoughts and feelings. The truth aligns you with The Process. When your understanding of anything is false or inaccurate, you're misaligned with what is, which causes suffering. Delusion or ignorance leads to suffering.

The reason that "Be present, bringing awareness and acceptance into every moment" is at the center of The Guidelines is because it enables every other guideline to be followed. Understanding the truth, communicating it selectively and skillfully is no exception. The only way you can follow this guideline is when you're present. There's so much information within The Process that our minds can't compute it all. We must be present to allow our connection to the intelligence within The Process to present us with the truth.

Feeling the truth

The Process rewards you with pleasant feelings when you understand the truth. Again, it may be subtle and can often be masked by other feelings or thoughts you are experiencing at the time. The pleasant feelings can be observed if you're sensitive enough to access them through your awareness. Even when you hear something truthful that your ego rejects, there will be an accompanying pleasant feeling. An example of this might be that you hear about a terminal diagnosis for yourself or a loved one. For most of us, this is going to create unpleasant feelings like anger, fear, worry or frustration. These feelings are triggered by our ego that doesn't want to understand or accept the truth. Once you really understand the truth and accept it, there will be a feeling of peace. Even if you know you are going to die soon. Until the point of acceptance, a part of your ego believes the diagnosis to be false. It's in resistance. This is where the delusion and unpleasant feelings come from. Sometimes, you experience other pleasant feelings like relief or appreciation because you're grateful to know what's actually happening.

Pleasant feelings relating to the truth may come about through the creation of stories within your head or through sensory input from what others are communicating. This might include reading a book, watching TV, listening to the radio, or listening to somebody who's speaking to you. This is why it makes sense to align yourself with truthful sources and move away from false sources. Reading books that contain the truth, like quality spiritual texts, will have a positive impact on you. Reading books that contain false statements will impact you negatively. An exception to this is fiction where you acknowledge that the story is fictional before reading it. Good fiction will contain truths within it. It's virtually impossible for newspapers or news channels to be truthful all of the time. However, some provide you with more truth than others, and you can feel the difference. Listening to people speaking the truth is nourishing. Listening to people who are speaking falsely is draining and unpleasant. Part of practicing this guideline is to take responsibility for what enters your senses, and to stay aware. With awareness you're much better placed to discriminate between what's true and false. Also, awareness shields you from suffering triggered by false communication from others.

When we're misaligned with the truth, it causes unpleasant feelings. These feelings will always be there, and sometimes they're very subtle. The unpleasant feelings are part of The Process's correction mechanism. Our bodies create unpleasant feelings when our thinking is deluded. This isn't bad. It's actually helpful. So long as we understand and respect it.

Keep in mind that the body is guiding you, and like all guides, it may be misinterpreted. For example, imagine a friend tells you something about yourself, which truthfully highlights some of your faults. If your ego doesn't like that, it will trigger emotional pain and unpleasant feelings within the body. If you're following this guidance literally or blindly, you might believe that what your friend is telling you is false, because of the unpleasant feelings you experience. In this case your friend is telling you the truth, but your ego believes what they are telling you is false! When you experience these unpleasant feelings, you know that something's misaligned within you. You're either believing what is true to be false; or believing what is false to be true. Either way, it's deluded thinking, which creates the unpleasant feelings. I'm sure you can recall times when this was the case; times when you created a great deal of suffering for yourself when you've misunderstood a situation.

The unpleasant feelings that are experienced when you're deluded link back to the guideline, "Be present, bringing awareness and acceptance into every moment." The unpleasantness is caused by your resistance to the truth. You resist something true by believing it's false; and you resist something false by believing it's true. Understanding what's true and false cultivates a peaceful mind – and helps you to accept situations. The mind may be deluded sometimes, but the body always knows the truth. That's why it responds the way it does. Utilizing its infinite intelligence, The Process uses the body as a feedback mechanism and a coach for the mind.

Determining the truth

The Yoga Sutras of Patanjali are ancient scriptures describing yoga practice and philosophy. Having studied various translations and commentaries, which I reference in the bibliography, I found plenty of guidance in there that helped inform and confirm The Guidelines. In the first of the four chapters, there's some useful advice on how to determine the truth. The various translations contain subtle differences in their explanations. My understanding is that Patanjali explains that for something to be confirmed as truthful, it must either be as a result of (i) direct perception (ii) inference or (iii) believing a trusted source.

> **Direct perception is when you know that something is true because you directly perceive it.**

If we see a field in front of us we know it's a field. If we feel the wind blowing against our face, we know it's windy. Direct perception is based on acknowledging facts. This is the most reliable way of understanding the truth because it's so direct. However, it's limited by what we can directly perceive, which is why we sometimes need to deploy the next two methods.

> **Inference involves using evidence and reasoning to confirm the truth.**

For example, if your alarm sounds in the morning, you can infer that it's time to wake up. If you look out of your window and see puddles everywhere, you can infer it's been raining. With this method, be careful not to jump to conclusions too early. If somebody spotted puddles on their drive, it may be their neighbor's water sprinkler that created them, rather than rain. If one person told you something about another, what they told you may not necessarily be true. Inferences that lead to the truth must be straightforward to understand. In complex situations, there are sometimes too many opportunities for a mistake to be made; then what you accept as the truth is actually false, or vice versa.

> **The third way of determining the truth is through using a trusted source.**

In the Yoga Sutras, the focus is on using a guru, or authoritative set of scriptures, to confirm spiritual truths. This method of understanding the truth can be applied in areas unrelated to spirituality. If you have a good friend that you trust, and they tell you about something they've observed, you can assume that to be the case. If you take your bicycle for repair to a specialist you trust, and they tell you it needs a new chain, you will believe them. This third method for determining the truth is similar to inference, in that it can be easily misused and lead to delusion. People often believe that somebody's a trusted source when that same person is speaking falsely. For example, a popular TV show with a longstanding reputation for truthful communication, may be proven to be false. Some sources are true sometimes and not others. Being present will help you determine which is which. Consistently true sources, which is what I believe Patanjali refers to, are rare, and should be cherished.

I've experienced my fair share of paranoia in the past and still do from time-to-time. Believing that people are out to get me when they've no intention of doing so. Creating stories in my mind that make me feel unpleasant again and again. I know many people experience the same. It's stressful, tiring, and ineffective. Believing in things that are untrue causes stress. When the mind's deluded it believes that The Process is different to how it actually is. The body is programmed to react to this by creating unpleasant feelings. When this happens, it's a sign that you're lost in thought, and have lost touch with the present moment.

I find the framework offered by Patanjali helps me to differentiate between facts, inference, or just some story I've created that may be false. I know from my own experience that the unpleasant stories I create hardly ever come true. The major challenges and difficulties I've experienced in life are usually the situations that I hadn't even anticipated.

A bi-product of determining the truth is confidence and strength of conviction. When you really understand yourself, another person, or a situation, the decisions you make along with any subsequent action are always aligned. This is real confidence that provides you with the inner-strength to act skillfully. It's very different to the false sense of confidence and vulnerability that people carry when their actions are based on false beliefs.

Being honest with yourself

The biggest opportunity to practice the guideline relating to truthfulness is to be honest with yourself. In particular, honest about your own needs, desires and aversions. Self-honesty is a prerequisite to self-kindness. It's only through acknowledging the truth about what you need and don't need, can you care for yourself fully. The only way you can be honest with others and understand the truth externally, is to know and accept yourself from within. Self-honesty also means understanding your own opinions and faults. By acknowledging these, you can be mindful of how they may be steering your thinking about people or situations.

People who are honest with themselves are better placed to skillfully express how they feel. They are usually straightforward to deal with, build good relationships, and demonstrate integrity. Because of their honesty and knowledge of their own faults, it makes it easier for others to trust and accept them. Wise people understand the concept of impermanence that's inherent within The Process. They acknowledge that even within themselves, everything is constantly changing. What's true about a person today may be false tomorrow.

The amount of honesty you have in relation to yourself is dependent upon the depth of your awareness. Somebody who is very aware will see deep into their minds and bodies. Through practicing the guideline on being present, your awareness can penetrate into your subconscious thoughts, giving you more insight into the workings of your whole mind and actions. Self-honesty is a reflection self-awareness. This is why we should empathize with people who cannot be honest with themselves, as it may be due to a lack of self-awareness. As their self-awareness develops, so will their honesty.

> Be compassionate to people when they're struggling to be honest about things, as they'll be suffering.

And be compassionate to yourself when you're in the same situation. Being honest with yourself enables acceptance. Failing to understand yourself, or believing something about yourself which is untrue, causes resistance and suffering. It manifests as indecisiveness, poor judgement, difficult relationships, and decisions that cause problems. The reason for the suffering is misalignment. Action is always faulty when it's based on deluded thinking. Remember that when we suffer psychologically, The Process is applying a correction. We're a small process within the big Process. The Process corrects the smaller processes it creates in the same way that a parent with good intentions corrects their children.

Communicating kindly and truthfully

To be aligned, your communication needs to be kind and truthful. Hence the emphasis on understanding the truth. Kindness is about being considerate, friendly and generous. When you're communicating kindly and truthfully, you're applying a combination of guidelines to align yourself. Communication is more than just speech. It includes all forms, such as written communication, digital communication, and body language. Paradoxically, not communicating is also a form of communication. What you don't communicate can be as impactful as what you do. The way we communicate influences how kind we are. We have to judge the best use of pace, tone and language. Where we communicate, and to whom we communicate with, must also be considered.

> **Firstly, and most importantly, to be kind, communication needs to be selective.**

When you communicate the truth without discernment you may cause harm. An obvious example of this is where you don't like somebody who likes you; and you tell them so. This would be communicating the truth, whilst at the same time being unkind. Imagine that a kind and sensitive friend of yours organized a vacation. After you returned, you formed an opinion that it was the least enjoyable vacation you'd been on in your entire life. The fact that you have this opinion is the truth. However, you would probably choose not to communicate it to your friend in such a direct way. There's always a time window between understanding the truth, and communicating it. Sometimes, you have the opportunity to stop and think about if you should communicate, and how to communicate. At other times, when you're already in communication with somebody, you may need to decide more dynamically in the moment. There's insufficient time to stop and analyze the situation. In these instances, follow the guideline on being present. It's only through the present moment, without being lost in thought, that you can communicate whatever truth is required at the time. This is required in highly complex situations, as your conscious mind isn't capable of taking everything into account. The infinite intelligence within The Process which you access when you're present, will guide the way.

Communicating part of the truth is often kinder, and more helpful, than communicating the whole truth. Somebody who wants to learn how to swim may go to a swimming instructor for lessons. The instructor will introduce the swimming techniques gradually. Giving the learner just what they need to build their confidence and make progress. Communicating part of the truth can also be sensitive and caring. If somebody asks you a question, and you know the whole truth is going to be harmful for them to hear, you can always share parts of the truth that you know will be easier for them to digest.

Keep in mind that not communicating is always an option. This comes in the form of silence for verbal communication. It appears in other forms like deciding not to respond to a digital message or keeping your eyes completely still.

> 99 A helpful rule of thumb that I follow – if I'm unsure about whether I should communicate, I won't communicate.

Often, people will ask me a question to which I don't have the answer. I'll look at them and remain in complete silence. Then, out of the silence may come some truthful and helpful communication. Silence helps us to connect to the intelligence within The Process. Stillness does the same. This is why people have been meditating for thousands of years. When you're in deep sleep, your body is still and your mind is still. This allows you to establish the connection, which is why you feel so nourished after having lots of deep sleep.

Whenever you communicate the truth with kindness, you're automatically considerate, friendly and generous. It may not always feel like this to the ego of the recipient. A child may ask their father to buy them a new toy they are already psychologically attached to having. If the father declines on the basis that the child already has enough toys, the child's ego may judge the father as behaving in an unfriendly way. They may even say, "I don't like you, I'm not your friend." This is the voice of the child's ego. Adults do things like this too. In this example, the father was considered, friendly and generous. The child's ego doesn't understand that the father's response will actually help them grow into a more aligned adult.

> 99 Be careful not to judge yourself on the basis of your ego or other people's egos.

This is especially true of those close to you like a partner, close friends or family members.

Paradoxically, I've experienced many situations where the truth has been spoken in a way that hasn't been particularly kind, but has resulted in kindness. I was out having dinner with a good friend of mine one evening. The waitress came over to bring us our bill and take payment. At many establishments these days, service staff are instructed to connect with the customer at a friendly and personal level. Many service staff greet their customers by asking what they've been doing earlier in the day. When the bill is being paid, they then ask what the customer is doing later when it's time to depart. On this occasion, my friend was using the credit card machine to pay the bill, and the waitress asked him, "So are you doing anything nice later then?" Whilst he was giving most of his attention to the credit card machine, he simply stated "No" and that ended the discussion. That made the waitress and I laugh. Subsequently, the three of us had a real friendly discussion, rather than a polite transactional exchange that was engineered by a customer service process.

Selective communication

Communicating kindly means selecting what you communicate. Communication can become more insightful, wise, and impactful, when you communicate less. Many people communicate whatever thoughts are active in their minds with no awareness or filtering. This is a sign of being lost in thought. It's unhelpful and harmful. A great deal of energy is wasted when people communicate in this way. For the person communicating and for the recipients.

> **If you tend to communicate too much, it's worth making a conscious effort to pause before communicating.**

Checking to see what you're planning to communicate is really necessary and helpful.

Communication contains a mixture of information and emotions. The recipient of your communication receives both. You color information in different ways through the active emotions at the time of communication. For example, you may be peaceful, angry, anxious or excited when you communicate. That energy will be shared with the recipient. Through managing your emotions and timing your communication, you can influence the emotional energy you transmit. Communicating kindly and selectively considers this emotional component.

Harmonious communication

Skillful communication of the truth will always promote harmony. Ultimately, this is about being in harmony with what The Process needs. One of the more visible applications is about cultivating harmony between people. The negative opposite to this, which is discouraged, is to communicate disharmoniously, which encourages divisiveness. I'm sure you would have experienced how good it feels to hear people talking kindly about others. And how unpleasant it is if you're on the receiving end of somebody gossiping negatively, or talking slanderously.

The reason truthful and harmonious communication works so well, is that it encourages people to become more aligned through being kind to each other. Divisive speech, which is often slanderous, encourages people to harm each other. As you can imagine, the immediate impact of this varies dependent upon the person communicating and their sphere of influence. People with leadership roles and responsibility for others should pay careful attention to this guideline as the impact of their communication is far reaching. That said, even if you don't consider yourself to be particularly influential, or responsible for things or people, you'll still have a huge impact with how you communicate.

> Pay careful attention to everything you communicate.

The butterfly effect demonstrates this where the tiny action of a butterfly flapping its wings can act as a catalyst to trigger a tornado. Everything's connected. A small amount of skillful communication to a single person has a positive ripple effect. Energy propagates.

Helping others find the truth through true listening

When teaching, I often say to people, "Your practice is *your* practice." You must be selective and conscious about trying to 'teach' people what I'm explaining in this book. Personally, the only time I find it helps to teach, is when people request a teaching; for instance, if somebody asks me a question, attends a talk I'm giving, or is reading something I've written. 'Teaching' people when they haven't asked for a teaching is not true teaching in the spiritual sense. It's intrusively forcing content onto somebody else without their permission. That said, there are ways you can teach others more indirectly, and one of those is by helping others find the truth for themselves through true listening. Most of us get plenty of opportunities to practice this; in person or through voice and video calls.

> 99 Practice true listening by following the guideline
> "Be present, bringing awareness and acceptance into
> every moment" as you listen to others.

It's beneficial for you and the person you're listening to. For you, it's like a meditation. You listen carefully to what the other person is saying without interrupting. As you listen, you bring awareness and acceptance to experiences within your mind and body: Thoughts, feelings, bodily sensations and form entering the senses. Whilst you're developing this practice, it may help you to direct a little awareness to something real in the body such as your breath or the energy in your hands. This anchors you to the present moment and prevents the mind from wandering off. If you catch yourself lost in thought, you can direct awareness to your body in order to regain mindfulness. This practice of true listening has an interesting effect on the person being listened to. For them, if you're present enough, it will feel as though you're holding a mirror up to their experience. They'll be able to experience their own thoughts, feelings, and bodily sensations, more clearly. This deeper awareness will then allow them to understand the truth that always comes from within.

You may have experienced this for yourself. You have been listened to by somebody who is very mindful and concentrated. It deepens your self-awareness. Interestingly, although true listening is positive, sometimes, it can leave the person who is being listened to feeling open and vulnerable. An active ego will be uncomfortable and feel threatened. The ego is always threatened when it's observed, because observation reduces it.

Young children who are still to develop their adult egos may perform the role of a true listener. Their minds are clear and not lost in self-referential thought. I remember a new partner and I driving around to the house where my children were living at the time. My son, who must have been around eight years old, appeared from the house and walked towards the car to say hello. It was the first time he had met her. They exchanged a few friendly words. Later on, after the visit, she told me that the encounter had felt like my son was looking into the depths of her soul! She was experiencing true listening.

True listening has another benefit. It prevents you from being harmed by the content of another's communication. When you're present, the mind only responds positively. If you find yourself in a situation where you have to listen to unskillful people, true listening becomes very important. Stay vigilant. Cultivating this skill enhances self-confidence and helps you manage relationships. When you're alone, being present and mindful is also a form of true listening. This type of true listening is listening to yourself. Listening to your own thoughts. You can also gain access to the truth in this way.

Skillful self-disclosure

Skillful communication includes skillful self-disclosure. How much should you communicate about yourself? When should you share your personal history, your ambitions, what you own, what you're connected with, what you're thinking and feeling? When deciding what to disclose, consider the following pointers:

- Your intention for disclosing personal information.
- Who you're disclosing personal information to.
- How the people you're communicating with may feel.
- The potential impact to yourself and others.

You might be disclosing things about yourself to manipulate your own self-image. I've done that many times due to low self-esteem. Most people don't know that when they first meet me because I display a confident front. When people have a self-esteem issue they either go overly negative or overly positive with the self-image they project. Some people may tell you how bad they are at something, or what big personal problems they've experienced, which is usually an inflation of the truth. Others may tell you that they're better than they actually are in some way. Again, an inflation of the truth. People with a balanced amount of self-esteem tend to be more truthful, straightforward and confident in their communication about themselves.

Inflating the truth is a form of lying. Even in a professional or business context. Another form of manipulating self-image is withholding the truth about yourself when it would actually be wiser and kinder to communicate it. People withhold the truth about themselves in an unskillful way when they're fearful. In the past, I've hidden my feelings due to being afraid of being judged as bad or weak. An even more obvious form of manipulating self-image is to lie blatantly. Sometimes, the further away from the truth you go the more harm you cause.

Once somebody lets go of projecting a false representation of who they are, their true self shines through, which is always beautiful. The true self is completely truthful and lives a life of harmony. The true self is fully aligned, because it's the intelligence within The Process. That's who we all are in our essence. We're one. Everything else about us changes including our thoughts and bodies. Ultimately, our sole purpose is to contribute towards the evolution of The Process. This could be on a grand scale, or by making small and valuable changes. Some people's contributions to spiritual evolution are more visible than others. However, the butterfly effect means that everybody's contribution is valuable and relatively equal. The true self is happy whatever we do; so long as it's aligned.

The Process contains the intelligence to help people know what they need to know to contribute towards the universe evolving, and act skillfully. Regardless of how much others withhold or distort information. That's why I tend not to interrogate people and situations too much to find things out. What I need to know, I'll know. When I need to know, I'll know. If I don't need to know, that's OK, I won't know.

Sometimes, what you disclose will be truthful and fact-based. Other times, it will be an opinion, and may be false. We can communicate untruthfully when we're experiencing feelings that we can't quite justify. We might tell people I'm feeling this because of that, when actually that may not be the case.

> If you're sharing opinions with others, rather than facts, it's worth communicating them as such.

Not just in relation to yourself, but in relation to people, and situations external to you. Caveating opinions as opinions is communicating truthfully and with consciousness.

Should you be completely open with people and disclose anything and everything? Disclosure should be selective and skillful. If you have time, you can work out what's skillful by checking your intention for the communication. If you're aware enough to realize that it's your ego controlling the communication to suit its agenda, then the communication will be unskillful. If you have positive and kind intentions then the communication will be skillful. We often don't have the time to think through this. Especially when we need to communicate with somebody there and then. When you're present, your self-disclosure and any kind of communication will be aligned.

>> A tactic you can use in challenging situations when you're
feeling at risk of saying something unskillful is to slow down.

Pause between your sentences. Pause between your words if you need to. I've never heard of people being forced to communicate at a certain speed. The worst that can happen is the person you're communicating with may feel a little concerned, suspicious, frustrated or uncomfortable if they're not used to silence. You're always best to say something slowly and skillfully, rather than fast and unskillfully.

When it's active, the ego can take over your communication. I experience this occasionally if I'm feeling anxious. Temporarily, I become completely selfish. Every aspect about my communication relates to what my ego desires. All consideration of others is temporarily lost. The end result is harm caused to those I'm communicating with, and feelings of guilt and regret afterwards. Even when we understand The Guidelines well, when we're lost in powerful emotions we can end up doing the opposite of what we know is right. We lose touch with our source of wisdom. People who are generally kind and wise, can temporarily lose it when experiencing potent emotions like anger, and communicate all sorts of harmful things. This is why the guideline about being present is so central to practice. It allows you to transcend these patterns, coming back to the truth, and back to what you know is good.

Skillful self-disclosure is particularly important in the area of digital and social media. We'll examine that in Chapter Nine – "Apply the guidelines to your digital device usage." All of the guidance above on self-disclosure applies equally to what you disclose about others including individuals and groups. Be responsible and kind with the knowledge that you hold. It's just as important to speak skillfully about others as it is about yourself.

Connections with other guidelines

All seven guidelines connect together, and support each other. The table on the following page highlights a few of the connections between "Understand the truth, communicating it selectively and skillfully," and the other guidelines.

Guideline	Connections
Honor the body	• Understanding the truth regulates feelings experienced within the body, which leads to better health. • Keeping the body in good condition helps you understand the truth. This is because the body acts as a conduit between The Process and the mind. • Honor the body by understanding the truth about what it needs and doesn't need.
Be present, bringing awareness and acceptance into every moment	• The guideline about truthfulness can only be followed when you're present. • Use your awareness of feelings within the body to help you understand what's true and false. • Only through knowing the truth can you truly accept a situation. • The amount of honesty you have in relation to yourself is dependent upon the depth of your self-awareness. • Being present is a way of enabling true listening – helping yourself and others to understand the truth. • You can use true listening as a mindfulness practice. • Being honest with yourself enables acceptance. Failing to understand yourself causes resistance and suffering.
Act with kindness, considering everyone and everything	• Communicating the truth selectively and skillfully is a form of kindness. • Kind communication of the truth is considerate, friendly and generous. • Communicating part of the truth may be the kind thing to do. • Honesty is a prerequisite to self-kindness. It's only through acknowledging the truth about what you need and don't need, can you care for yourself fully. • Spread kindness to others by communicating harmoniously. • Protect yourself from the content of another's communication through true listening. • Be kind to others by helping them understand the truth through true listening. • Skilful disclosure about yourself and others is an act of kindness. • Be responsible and kind with the knowledge that you hold. It's just as important to speak skillfully about others as it is about yourself.
Do only what needs to be done	• Consider letting go of spending time with people who consistently speak falsely. • Let go of accessing sources of false information. • Communicate selectively, only when it's needed, to whom it's needed and where it's needed. • Offer spiritual teachings only when you're asked to do so.
Harmoniously obtain and retain only what you need	• Be honest with yourself about what you really need and let go of what you don't need.

Guideline	Connections
Apply The Guidelines to your digital device usage	• Access digital content you believe to be true. • Let go of accessing digital content that you believe to be false. • Be selective about how much you communicate using digital means and who you communicate with. • Skillful disclosure of your personal information and the information of others is particularly important in the areas of digital communication including social media.

You can find a list of ideas for practicing this guideline in the final chapter "Building & Structuring Your Practice."

POINTS FOR REFLECTION

1. Understanding the truth will always bring about a peaceful acceptance of any situation.

2. We must be present to allow our connection to the intelligence within The Process to present us with the truth.

3. You resist something true by believing it's false; and you resist something false by believing it's true.

4. For something to be confirmed as truthful, it must either be as a result of direct perception, inference or believing a trusted source.

5. When the mind's deluded it believes The Process is different to how it actually is, which causes stress.

6. A bi-product of determining the truth is confidence and strength of conviction.

7. Self-honesty is a prerequisite to self-kindness.

8. It's only through the present moment, without being lost in thought, that you can communicate whatever truth is required at the time.

9. You can teach others indirectly, by helping them find the truth for themselves through true listening. True listening also prevents you from being harmed by the content of another's communication.

10. Skillful communication of the truth will always be harmonious with what The Process needs.

11. If you have time, you can work out what's skillful by checking your intention for the communication.

12. You're always best to say something slowly and skillfully, rather than fast and unskillfully.

Chapter Seven

Do Only What Needs
to Be Done
Stated negatively: Do not do what is unnecessary

THE PROCESS OFFERS YOU opportunities on how to spend your time; ranging from your simple daily activities, through to more substantial areas like career and relationships. You make hundreds of decisions about what to do every day.

Each decision is an opportunity to be creative and align yourself to what's really needed, rather than what your ego wants. When following The Guidelines, decisions are made by keeping this mantra in mind: "Do only what needs to be done."

Guideline: Do Only What Needs to Be Done

The global epidemic of being busy

The norm in this day and age is for people to do too much; keeping themselves busy. You may observe this when you speak with people. You ask how somebody's doing and they say, "I've been busy." Businesses are following the same trend. As the push continues for economic performance, businesses are expecting increased productivity from their workforce. I've heard the word 'busy' increase significantly over the last few years. It's now culturally normal for people to be busy and identify with being busy. I appreciate I'm generalizing here, and that there are many people, maybe even yourself, who don't fit within this category and lead more spacious lives.

Sometimes it's right to be busy, but when you're *excessively busy*, you're busier than you need to be. The problem with being excessively busy is that generally speaking, people find it harder to stay present. Because being present is at the center of The Guidelines, the more people are excessively busy, the more they'll be misaligned and unskillful. It's always the excess activity that causes the problems.

There's a relationship between being busy and consuming more, which relates to the guideline in the next chapter "Harmoniously obtain and retain only what you need." The more stuff you acquire, the more money you need to pay for it all. Time and energy are required to acquire new things, and maintain what you currently have. Things people own are replaced in the name of style and fashion long before they've reached the end of their useful life. Economic pressure works against us here. You switch on the news and hear, "We've had a good quarter in the retail sector – people have been getting out and spending – consumer confidence is high, which is really helping." New fashions and trends are being advertised at breakneck speed to encourage people to consume more.

If the human species wishes to extend its existence it will need to deal with this growing cultural issue of people over-consuming, and being excessively busy. There are two ways this can be tackled. The first is through international agreements between countries. These are extremely challenging to design, negotiate, implement and sustain. Mainly because countries have their own economic and power-based agendas. The other way such changes come about are through individuals across the globe collectively taking positive action; thinking more creatively and making changes to how much they do, without being influenced so much by external sources with financial and power-based agendas.

It's my hope, that through spiritual teachings becoming more mainstream, and people gaining more knowledge about how The Process works, things will change. The global collective will start consuming less and doing less. People will become more content with simplicity and what is. Craving and suffering will reduce. Countries will let go of their need for power. This is the vision. If things continue as they have been doing, the human species will accelerate towards its own extinction. If we follow The Guidelines, and other quality spiritual teachings, humans will be around for much longer. Either way, at some point we will become extinct. We can count on that because everything is created, sustained and then destroyed.

Reviewing your activities

Doing only what needs to be done, involves aligning your activities with The Guidelines.

> **Review your existing activities by creating a list of everything you do.**

Be sure to include your digital activities e.g. social media, emailing, and watching online videos. Work through each activity following the process below:

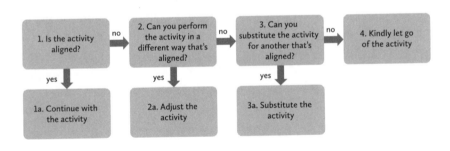

Reviewing Existing Activities

The first step is to determine whether the activity is aligned (step 1) using the list of guidelines on the following page. Reviewing existing activities requires a good understanding of The Guidelines. If you're reading this book sequentially you may choose to return to this exercise and finish it once you have a better understanding of the final two guidelines covered in Chapters Eight and Nine.

Guideline stated positively	Guideline stated negatively
Honor the body	Do not harm the body
Be present, bringing awareness and acceptance into every moment	Do not become lost in thought
Act with kindness, considering everyone and everything	Do not be intentionally harmful or single-minded in your actions
Understand the truth, communicating it selectively and skillfully	Avoid excessive, harmful and false communication
Do only what needs to be done	Do not do what is unnecessary
Harmoniously obtain and retain only what you need	Do not obtain or retain more than you need
Apply The Guidelines to your digital device usage	Do not disregard The Guidelines in your digital device usage

The Guidelines

If the activity you're reviewing is aligned, then continue with it (step 1a). If not, you may be able to adjust the activity in some way to ensure alignment (step 2). Let's take an example relating to honoring the body. Consider somebody who's running excessively to the point where they're damaging their knees. An adjustment may be to lower the intensity and exercise safely. That activity then becomes aligned, and may be continued. Ensuring alignment is not just about *what* you do. It's also about *how* you do it. You'll be surprised at how many misaligned activities can be adjusted and aligned through being creative. Back to the previous example, if adjustments to running were impossible, then the activity may be substituted (step 3). In this case, the runner may switch to cycling, which places less strain on the joints. If the runner damaged their body to the extent that they couldn't undertake any form of exercise at all for a while, they would need to temporarily let go of exercising (step 4).

You may have noticed the word *kindly* in step 4 of the process diagram: "Kindly let go of the activity."

> We should let go of activities with consideration and kindness.

Letting go of significant addictive activities is challenging. With some addictions, completely stopping the activity without a substitute or expert advice is harmful. In these cases, releasing the addiction will need to be approached in a way that you minimize the harm caused – you approach it kindly. Letting go of activities that involve others should be done so in a way that's sensitive to them. Applying the guidelines, "Understand the truth, communicating it selectively and skillfully" and "Be present, bringing awareness and acceptance into every moment" are relevant and helpful. They can be difficult to apply though; especially in instances where you're craving to let go as quickly as possible. Patience and care are required.

> **It's always worth exploring adjustments and substitutions prior to letting go of an activity.**

Many activities are partially aligned. Let's say that you talk in a way that's unkind and slanderous whilst spending time with a friend. On the face of it, you might say that spending time with that friend is misaligned. However, if you examine the situation closely, you may find that you're also being kind to yourself. It may be that you need connection with others and companionship, which this friendship provides. The adjustment and substitution steps involve analyzing the activity; understanding which components of it are aligned and which components are misaligned. When you do look for adjustments or substitutions you aim to retain the aligned components, and let go of the misaligned components. In this example, you may make an adjustment by agreeing a pledge to speak harmoniously together. That's a great adjustment as it helps you and your friend become more aligned.

When you let go of activities, it can be tempting to add new ones that refill your time.

> **Try using some of your free time to undertake your remaining activities more mindfully.**

Generally speaking, it's easier to bring awareness and acceptance to every moment when you go slower. Consider the world's most influential spiritual teachers. Have you ever observed them rushing around, or speaking quickly?

Free time and doing less may bring up emotional pain that's been suppressed. If this happens, give the pain space, awareness and acceptance. Allow yourself to heal. Even on vacation, some people end up filling their time doing as much as possible. Many people are incessantly busy because they're incapable of releasing the emotional pain they're carrying around in their bodies. The excess activities are used as a coping mechanism to protect them – this is natural.

During the initial review, you may end up with a long list of activities to consider and change. If this is the case, prioritize. Start with a few easy changes as these will build confidence and motivation. Then move onto releasing or substituting activities that have the potential to cause the most suffering. Don't get too caught up in the prioritization though. The main thing is that you're making positive changes. Reviewing activities using the process above is an ongoing exercise as you'll be adding and changing activities throughout your whole life.

As a rule of thumb, you can run this exercise monthly to begin with; and then reduce the frequency to quarterly or annually once you're more aligned. Aligning yourself with The Guidelines usually takes years. Even the most dedicated practitioners may be working on it for the whole of their lives.

Aligning new activities

Reviewing your activities using the approach described in the previous section is helpful. To stay aligned with this guideline, you also need to be diligent with every new opportunity that's presented to you – big or small. This is achieved by being present, and creating space between the opportunity and decision to act. The simple activity of cleaning provides a good illustration of this. You spot some dirt or dust in your home, which presents you with an opportunity to clean. If you're completely obsessive with cleaning, you'll simply pick up a cloth or duster, and get onto it right away. It can be addictive in that there's no choice involved. Instead, the ideal would be that there's a pause, and you ask yourself, "Does this really need to be cleaned now?" If it does, then clean it. If it doesn't, then do it later when it really needs to be done. Get into the habit of pausing, even if it's briefly, before every activity and then asking yourself whether it really needs to be done. Is everything you do really needed? Or are you doing things out of habit from your past conditioning? Do only what needs to be done.

Prioritizing your activities whilst being present

Given the range of opportunities we have for different activities and the cultural pressure many of us face to get involved in lots of things, it's helpful to prioritize activities. This may involve making a prioritized list as discussed earlier. Certain elements of the prioritization are simple. For example, if you've got a major health issue that needs urgent attention, it makes sense to prioritize that above doing the cleaning. At other times, prioritization is more complex; even if all of the activities you've listed are aligned.

> It's worth reading the list of guidelines, and keeping them in mind, when you prioritize your activities.

The Guidelines will direct you. Being present during the prioritization process rather than being lost in thought is essential. This will enable you to use the intelligence from within The Process for guidance. Using this intelligence is the only way you can truly prioritize, as it takes everything and everyone into account. When you're lost in thought, your ego, or constrained sense of self will be doing the work, based on its own selfish desires, aversions and past conditioning. Your mind isn't capable of taking the universe into account and being truly creative by itself.

Prioritizing activities whilst being Present is acting with kindness to everyone and everything. It allows you to balance prioritizing what The Process has made you personally responsible for, with a wider perspective and consideration of everything else. Through this approach, you're allowing The Process to adjust itself and evolve through you. Surrendering to that is life's true purpose.

On a more practical level, to ensure you're present, undertake your prioritization in a place, and at a time, when you'll be peaceful and concentrated. Allow sufficient time. Fifteen minutes of quality time will usually be enough. I prioritize every Sunday to set me up for the following week.

> Consider finding a regular slot and including a reminder in your diary, to help you get into the habit of prioritizing.

Karma yoga

The Bhagavad Gita, a popular Hindu and yoga scripture, has a lot to say about activities that need to be done – 'the what.' In addition, it provides guidance on how we should do them – 'the how.' The teachings describe a practice called *karma yoga*, which is undertaking activities unselfishly without being attached to the results. The related teachings in The Gita integrate beautifully with other teachings in this book, providing a useful lens on the guideline, "Do only what needs to be done."

Another name for karma yoga is 'selfless service.' This means more than just serving other people. If you're watering a plant for the sake of the plant, without any personal expectation from the results of the action, that's karma yoga. When you remove an insect from your house with the intention of giving it freedom without expecting anything for yourself, that's karma yoga. Any kind action taken when you're unattached to the results is karma yoga. Karma yoga is always aligned with the needs of The Process. There's a clue that points to this, in the name 'selfless service.' There's no self! When you're practicing karma yoga you're free from selfish desire. The action is free from the false sense of self, another name for the ego. Karma yoga can only be performed when you're present – connected to the intelligence within The Process; free from the selfish meddling of the ego. When you are free from the ego, your activities are non-competitive. Karma yoga is at the altruistic end of the Selfishness/Altruism Intention Scale introduced in Chapter Five. The opposite to karma yoga is selfish action, completely driven by the ego with no altruistic motivation.

You can have an expectation in relation to an activity without being attached to the outcome. An expectation is a belief that something will happen. Occasionally, when my children were young, I'd offer them helpful advice on various matters, expecting them to do what I suggested. I know this was a form of karma yoga on some occasions, because if they didn't follow the advice, I'd remain peaceful. I had an expectation but wasn't attached to it. Occasionally, I'd become frustrated if they didn't follow the advice I was giving them. When this happened, this was not karma yoga, as I was personally attached to the result – hence the suffering. When you're unattached from the results of your actions, you gain freedom from the anxiety associated with how things turn out. It's liberating; making activities and achieving goals far more enjoyable.

I particularly enjoy observing others practicing karma yoga, even when they've never heard about the teaching. You can observe people carrying out random acts of kindness, without any selfish desire or expectation involved. It might be helping somebody less mobile across the road, or removing a snail from the sidewalk and placing it somewhere safe without expecting anything in return. Even relatively small actions are a form of karma yoga when undertaken without attachment to the results.

Many ashrams offer people opportunities for karma yoga practice. This often takes the form of work that contributes towards the maintenance and general running of the place. It can include activities like cleaning, cooking or performing administrative duties. In return, the karma yogis, those doing the work, may be provided with food and accommodation for their services. If your main motive for doing this is to tell people how spiritual you are, or to get some free accommodation in a place you find pleasurable, that's not karma yoga. Even although it may be badged as karma yoga. That said, joining karma yoga programmes with selfish motives may still be spiritually beneficial. Whether these activities are true karma yoga, is dependent upon the mindset of those doing them. True karma yoga is determined by intention, not by the type of activity you do. The reality is that there will often be a mixture of motives. People are operating somewhere on the continuum of the Selfishness / Altruism Intention Scale.

Karma yoga is often explained as action you dedicate to a higher power or God. Mapping this onto the teachings in this book is straightforward. When you practice karma yoga, you do so to align with or serve The Process. This is why karma yoga activities are always rewarding. They feel good after you've completed them. The Process is rewarding you for acknowledging it and following its guidelines.

One of the reasons karma yoga has the name it does is that it neutralises existing karma, and doesn't create any new karma. By practicing karma yoga, suffering associated with unskillful actions from the past can surface, providing the opportunity to accept and release it. You're giving The Process the opportunity to correct you for your wrongdoings. I've experienced this a lot myself. I'll be doing something for somebody without any expectations or wanting anything in return; with no involvement from my ego. It might be helping a friend move house, or going out to the shop to buy somebody a gift. Occasionally, during the activity, especially if it's a simple activity, I'll experience emotional pain from the past and unpleasant thoughts. People carrying less negative karma find it easier to be truly generous. They aren't prone to suffer as much during acts of generosity. In fact, they usually enjoy generous activities. The more karma somebody carries, the larger their ego, making them more likely to act with selfish intentions. This makes karma yoga challenging. Karma yoga by its nature is generous. Generosity is a component of kindness, which reinforces the link with the guideline, "Act with kindness, considering everyone and everything."

The Gita claims that through practicing karma yoga you'll be provided with everything you need. Believing this allays the fear of becoming diminished or losing out through serving others. This type of fear can show itself in the form of a scarcity mentality; or a fear that you'll get depressed through practicing karma yoga as you won't be experiencing enough pleasure. The truth is that karma yoga activities have the potential to be very enjoyable.

The teaching about being provided with everything you need can be validated. To serve others effectively, you also need to look after yourself and ensure your own needs are met. The two are inseparable. You can take responsibility for getting your own needs met for the indirect benefit of others.

> Dedicate action you take to meet your own needs for the benefit of serving others.

Over time with spiritual practice, your personal desires reduce as your service to others increases. Wants are optional and egoic. You may want a new coat when you already have a coat that's sufficient for your needs. The ego says, "Go on, treat yourself to that new coat, you deserve it." Needs are different to wants. Needs are what's required to maintain yourself optimally to follow The Guidelines. They're required to maintain your health and well-being. You need a coat to stay dry or warm. I must say that this example is for illustrative purposes. There may well be times when you do genuinely need to buy a new coat!

Karma yoga is aligned perfectly with the guidelines because of the link, to "Act with kindness, considering everyone and everything." True kindness consists of no attachment to the fruits of your actions. You simply act with positive intentions and trust that The Process takes good care of what happens subsequently.

Is this really necessary?

Many people get involved in more things than is necessary and then complain about being too busy.

> By filtering our activities and doing less of what's unnecessary, we end up doing more from a spiritual standpoint.

We create more peace and harmony in our lives. How do we determine what's a necessary and unnecessary activity? By reviewing it with questions relating to each of The Guidelines. Asking ourselves questions like:

- Is this honoring the body?
- Will doing this help me stay present?

- Is this activity kind?
- Do I really need to communicate this?
- Do I really need these things that I'm spending time and energy acquiring?
- Is using my digital device really necessary right now?

Asking questions like these is a powerful way of aligning yourself. Over time it becomes second nature. I keep these questions in a note stored on my phone. If ever I'm unsure about whether I should be doing something, I'll ask myself the questions. It soon becomes clear as to whether I should continue with the activity, adjust it, substitute it or let go of it.

Some of your activities may need to reduce in frequency. Especially where you observe them causing harm. Exercising more than the body needs is an example of this. Another example would be initiating sex as an escape from boredom or emotional pain when the body doesn't actually need it. We may socialize in person or online more than we need to. When we do things to excess, we're being driven by our egos rather than what The Process needs, which links to addictions.

Addictions are one of the biggest contributors to unnecessary activity. People spend so much time doing things they're addicted to and many of them don't even know they have the addictions. We can be spending time doing things, consuming things and thinking things in auto-pilot mode. Simply repeating what we've done in the past to distract ourselves from unpleasant feelings.

> Working to release our addictions, and healing the emotional pain that causes them, is necessary for us to become more aligned.

Activities that help release addictions are acts of kindness as they help you become more present and peaceful.

The near enemy of letting go of activities is doing so little that you fail to take care of your own needs. Sitting around not doing anything and feeling depressed; feeling sorry for yourself and miserable, is not following The Guidelines. You do need to take responsibility for doing things to meet your needs. Again, this is a form of kindness. If you really need to do something, you should do it.

Treading your own unique path

The Process is configured so that everybody has their own unique path. You respect this by being true to yourself, and what you need to do. This is doing what needs to be done. When you don't tread your own path and compete with the path of others, you cause yourself and others stress. The ego's responsible for competitiveness. When we're in touch with who we truly are and connected to the intelligence of The Process, we follow our own unique path that has been carefully designed to optimize our personal evolution; and to contribute to the evolution of The Process overall. This links together nicely with the guideline, "Understand the truth, communicating it selectively and skillfully." To understand our own unique path is to understand the truth. Note that the type of competitiveness I'm referring to here is about our paths in life. Competitiveness in areas like sport, business, or succeeding in a job interview are fine, so long as you're doing these things for positive reasons and not deliberately causing harm.

Have you ever observed somebody who's competing with somebody else's path? Wanting to beat them or get level with them in some way? Maybe you've done this yourself. I know I have. The unpleasant feelings people experience when they do this is feedback from The Process; informing them of misalignment. I must point out that it's fine to take inspiration and ideas from people and apply those in your own life. This helps you progress and achieve goals. But when you're trying to be better than somebody to feed your own ego it always causes problems. Energy used in egoic activities from these pursuits is contaminated. I recall a friend of mine going into a sun tanning shop and burning her breasts and backside. Initially, she wasn't too sure why she even went there. After some reflection, it turned out that subconsciously she wanted to have a darker sun tan than a work colleague who had just returned from vacation!

Many dysfunctional thought patterns including those that cause us to compete with another's path, operate at a subconscious level. Competitiveness always starts with egoic comparison. Egoic comparison is flawed because it works on an invalid assumption that people are separate. It doesn't see the truth, which is that we're all connected and part of one entity – The Process. When you truly understand that, comparisons and competitiveness drop away naturally. They're replaced by a loving appreciation of yourself and everybody around you. The more we practice awareness, the more these dysfunctional thought patterns can be observed, understood and substituted with the truth.

Working within The Guidelines

The majority of us will spend a large percentage of our time at work. If you have a job, it needs to be closely examined to check for alignment; what you do and how you do it.

> **Determine if your work is aligned by reviewing it against The Guidelines.**

Here are some pointers:

- Ensure your work is kind to yourself and others. Avoid or at least minimize any harm being caused. Avoid jobs that contribute to encouraging harm and promoting activities that are misaligned.
- Your work needs to be compatible with honoring the body. Basic needs should be met including exercise, rest, sleep and right diet. Your work shouldn't harm your body.
- Your work should allow you to communicate truthfully, skillfully and straightforwardly. Jobs that encourage any form of lying or manipulation should be avoided.
- The income earned from your work needs to be sufficient to enable you to obtain and retain what you need.
- If your job contains a digital element as most jobs do these days, then check alignment with the guideline, "Apply The Guidelines to your digital device usage."

Communication and thoughts

"Do only what needs to be done," can relate to communication. The guideline, "Understand the truth, communicating it selectively and skillfully" points to this. Selective communication means having the discernment to communicate whenever it's needed and only when it's needed. When you communicate unnecessarily, energy is being used to cause harm rather than to be kind and helpful. Paradoxically, if you don't communicate when you need to, the excess energy will be channeled unskillfully. This happens when you fail to tell somebody how you feel, and then complain about them not understanding you.

At an even subtler level we can link, "Do only what needs to be done" with our thoughts. Most people think far more than they need to. They become lost in their own thoughts and lose their awareness. It's like dreaming.

When we think in this way we're losing vital energy, and the thoughts we have are always problematic and misaligned. When we're present and practicing the guideline, "Be present, bringing awareness and acceptance into every moment," we only think when we need to and enjoy a peaceful mind.

Consideration of others

'Doing only what needs to be done' considers the whole – not just the individual. I'll give you an example. Let's assume for a moment that you're in a relationship and your partner would like you to go on vacation with them. Let's also assume that you don't need a vacation; you'd prefer to stay home. Even although you don't need a vacation yourself, you may still choose to go along as an act of kindness to your partner. And you might enjoy it when you do. Even if you don't personally need to do something, you can still do it for others if it's not going to cause any harm. That falls under the category of doing what needs to be done. Parents of small children practice this sometimes. They get involved in activities to entertain their children. The parents don't personally need to do the activity, but because they have parental responsibility they get involved for the benefit of their children. Sometimes the parents enjoy the activity. Sometimes they don't. Either way, it's an act of kindness.

Most of us have responsibilities like personal relationships, friendships, family, pets, work and so on. It's our duty to honor obligations that The Process has presented us with, so we need to consider them as part of our practice. Rather than just considering ourselves, we consider others who relate to our obligations. If we're finding it difficult to fulfil our obligations then we must ask ourselves why, and what needs to change.

Connections with other guidelines

All seven guidelines connect together, and support each other. The table below highlights a few of the connections between, "Do only what needs to be done" and the other guidelines.

Guideline	Connections
Honor the body	• Establish the right balance of activities to give the body what it needs. • Don't harm the body by giving it what it doesn't need.

Guideline	Connections
Be present, bringing awareness and acceptance into every moment	• Prioritizing your activities whilst being present is acting with kindness to everyone and everything. • Check that any new activities you undertake are aligned by staying present. Use the space between the opportunities presented to you and your decision to take those opportunities. • You must be present when practicing karma yoga. • Practicing awareness deeply gives you access to your subconscious thought patterns. They can highlight addictions and the ego operating at subtle levels. • When you're present, you only think when you really need to.
Act with kindness, considering everyone and everything	• Kindly let go of misaligned activities. • Prioritizing activities whilst being Present is acting with kindness to everyone and everything. • Karma yoga consists of acts of kindness with no attachment to the outcomes. • True kindness contains no attachment to the fruits of your actions. • Karma yoga by its nature, is a form of generosity. • Karma yoga is aligned perfectly with the guidelines because of the link to "Act with kindness, considering everyone and everything." • Activities for the benefit of others, rather than your ego's desires, are acts of kindness. • Activities that help release your addictions are aligned, as they are acts of kindness. • Take responsibility for doing things to meet your needs. This is a form of kindness. If you really need to do something, you should do it. • Cultivate a mindset of dedicating action you take to meet your own needs for the benefit of serving others, as well as yourself.
Understand the truth, communicating it selectively and skilfully	• Doing what needs to be done applies to communication as much as to activities. Communicate selectively. • To understand your own unique path is to understand the truth.
Harmoniously obtain and retain only what you need	• Activity is required to acquire new things and maintain what you currently have. Obtaining only what you need, and letting go of what you don't need, helps you let go of excessive doing.
Apply The Guidelines to your digital device usage	• Include your digital activities within any activity reviews. Especially those which are big time and energy consumers. Review your social media usage, and ask yourself if it's all really needed. • If your job contains a digital element, then check alignment with the guideline, "Apply The Guidelines to your digital device usage" in Chapter Nine.

You can find a list of ideas for practicing this guideline in the final chapter "Building & Structuring Your Practice."

POINTS FOR REFLECTION

1. Excess activities should be let go of with consideration and kindness.

2. It's always worth exploring adjustments and substitutions prior to letting go of an activity.

3. Sometimes it's right to be busy. When you're *excessively busy*, you're busier than you really need to be, and will find it harder to stay present.

4. There's a relationship between consuming more and being busy.

5. Consider finding a regular slot and including a reminder in your diary, to help you get into the habit of prioritizing your activities.

6. When you're unattached from the results of your activities, you gain freedom from the anxiety associated with how things will turn out.

7. Addictions are one of the biggest contributors to unnecessary activity.

8. Sitting around not doing anything and feeling depressed; feeling sorry for yourself and miserable, is not following The Guidelines.

9. If you really *need* to do something, you should do it.

10. We can link, "Do only what needs to be done" with our thoughts. Most people think far more than they need to.

11. It's our duty to honor obligations The Process has presented us with.

Harmoniously Obtain and Retain Only What You Need

Stated negatively: Do not obtain or retain more than you need

THE PROCESS KNOWS exactly what items you need at any given time to live harmoniously. This ranges from large items like a home, to smaller items like clothing. It also includes digital items like the apps you've got installed on your phone, and information stored on your computer. When you obtain and retain only what's needed, you live harmoniously. If you do otherwise, The Process will correct you at some point in the future. You'll experience the correction anytime, from the moment after you've taken more than you need, to years later. Corrections may also be applied in future lifetimes.

Guideline: Harmoniously Obtain and Retain Only What You Need

The Process isn't evolved enough to ensure that everybody has just what they need, and no more. Because of this, the responsibility is with us to decide what we need to acquire, retain and let go of. What everybody needs is different. You may need a large home; whilst your friend needs a small home. Your friend may need a particular book; you may not need that same book. Our needs change over time. Change and impermanence makes applying The Guidelines a real-time, lifelong practice.

> **To align with this guideline, apply the three simple rules below.**

I'll explain more about these in the following sections.
1. *Let go* of what you don't need.
2. *Retain* what you already have, and do need.
3. *Harmoniously obtain* what you need, but don't have.

Reviewing your items

The Process takes all of your items into account. I'll list a few examples to illustrate what I mean by items: properties, cars, clothes, books, phones, laptops, watches, tools, plants, furniture, crockery, exercise equipment, toiletries, cosmetics, food, bicycles, digital items e.g., apps and files. If you think about all the things you own, I'm sure you'll be able to add to this list.

> **Reviewing your items regularly, maybe once per quarter, will help you become more aligned.**

Reviewing your items takes time. Even for people with a modest amount of stuff. Breaking the task down into chunks works well. The easiest way to do this is to take one area at a time. For example: Living room, dining room, kitchen, bathroom, bedroom, office, garage, phone, laptop. You then have the option of spreading the task over a number of days. For each area, decide what to retain and what to let go of. Inevitably, for certain items, the decision and process of letting go will be challenging. Being present with the item and asking yourself the following questions, will help inform your decision:

- Why do I need this?
- When was the last time I used this?
- Will I definitely need this in the future?

- Does this have sentimental value?
- Is retaining this really helping me?
- Does this trigger certain feelings within me?
- Can I sell this and use the proceeds for something more worthwhile?
- How much space is this taking up?

For each item you plan to let go of, be clear about the next steps. Will you donate it, sell it, give it away, or put it in the trash? When things cannot be released immediately, create yourself a to-do list with a completion date. Slowly but surely, over time, you'll own less and may benefit from:

- More physical space.
- Less to manage, clean and maintain.
- A clearer more peaceful mind – owning less means there's less to think about.
- Extra cash generated from selling items.
- Opportunities to be generous when you give stuff away or sell it cheaply.

It feels great when you've de-cluttered and let go of things you don't really need. This is because in doing so, you're aligning yourself with The Guidelines. The Process arranges for your body to reward you with pleasant feelings when you're taking action to become more aligned.

> **We should practice kindness to others when letting go of items.**

For a while, I had two homes in England. One in Nottingham where my children were based, and the other in Bournemouth. For most of the time, I was living alone. Across the two properties I had three bathrooms, five bedrooms, three living rooms, two kitchens and a garden – all for one person! For a while, I was unaware of the fact that I had more than I needed. I'd regularly complain to myself about having two places to fund and maintain. One day, I remember waking up to the excessiveness – feeling greedy and uncomfortable about the situation. My immediate reaction was to sell the property in Nottingham. I knew it needed to go at some point.

I decided to retain it whilst my son was stopping with me at weekends. He'd been doing that since he was young, when his mother and I separated.

We had lovely times together. I enjoyed looking after him, and taking him breakfast in bed on a Sunday morning. When he reached around sixteen years old he was quite happy to stay with his mother during weekend evenings. Once I knew it would be OK with my son, I sold the house in Nottingham. Letting go of it felt great. Sometimes, you need to consider others and be patient when letting go of things. Even if it means accepting inconvenience and challenges for yourself in the process.

> Be kind to yourself when you're letting go of things.

If you believe that letting go of something will be harmful to you, then consider retaining it for a while longer. Temporary inconvenience or discomfort is fine when letting go of things. However, when you believe it will cause harm or emotional pain, review your approach. It may be that you need to let go of the item later, or in a different way. How we let go of items is as important as what we let go of.

Somebody might tell themselves they don't really need their TV. If they're addicted to watching TV, and worry they'll feel depressed without it, then it's probably best for them to retain it for a while longer. If they did want to be free of it, they could slowly reduce their viewing hours over a few weeks. And then let go of the TV when they feel more confident that they'd be fine without it.

Harmoniously obtain only what you need

An important part of this guideline is taking responsibility for obtaining what you need. We all need things. As I mentioned earlier, it depends on the person and the point in time, as to what those things are.

> If you get your needs met you'll be peaceful. If you don't get what you need, you'll suffer.

It's a simple equation. We all need healthy food. If we don't get healthy food we suffer physically. We need other basic necessities like shelter and clothes to wear. These types of basic needs are common for all people. Some needs are tailored to our own personal circumstances. Somebody with five young children will need a home that provides enough space for them. You may have a physical condition that means your body needs certain medication.

We need items that allow us to follow the guideline, "Do only what needs to be done." If you have a job, you'll need things to equip yourself for work. If you have responsibility for a pet dog, you'll need balls and a lead. The reason I'm providing these simple examples is to make the point that this guideline is not about letting go of things to the point where you can't fulfil your responsibilities. Quite the opposite. It's about taking responsibility for ensuring you have the items that enable you to meet obligations to yourself and others. And it's also about letting go of items that hinder you from meeting those obligations.

"Harmoniously obtain and retain only what you need," starts with the word 'harmoniously' for good reason. In the process of obtaining things, you need to be kind to yourself, and others who may be involved. Kindness helps to harmonize you with what The Process needs. And it increases the probability that obtaining things will be a smooth process. Here are a few pointers:

- **Only take things when they're freely given.** Never when somebody is unwilling to give them to you. Taking anything from people who are reluctant to give, including their time or energy, is a form of stealing.

- **Be straightforward with people.** Never use manipulative tactics to obtain things – this would be disregarding the guidelines on truthfulness and kindness. Attempting to have somebody sell you something for a price lower than they'd be comfortable with is an example of this.

- **Only obtain what you can genuinely afford.** If you believe that getting yourself into debt to obtain something will be harmful, reconsider whether you should have it.

- **Be kind to yourself and others, in the process of earning money.** Sometimes people cause themselves harm by working excessively, or working in unethical environments to earn money to purchase things. If this is the case, either go without the item or find a more ethical and kinder way of earning the money to pay for it. Be kind to others, and save yourself a lot of stress by earning money in an honest and straightforward way.

- **Obtain things that have been ethically produced or sourced.**
Consuming unethically sourced products or services is encouraging
their harmful production. Sourcing ethically produced products
and services is an appreciation of kindness.

- **Go for quality.** Items created mindfully and ethically, are the ideal
things to source. They have a wonderful quality to them. They
look beautiful, feel beautiful, and work beautifully. Most of the
time, high quality items last far longer than their lower quality
equivalents. They justify the additional expenditure. A friend of
mine says, "Buy cheap, buy twice!" One of the reasons people
purchase cheap low-quality items is because they know they'll
replace them once fashions change. When people only obtain
what they need, rather than being greedy, they have more funds
available to purchase higher quality items. When quality items are
used mindfully, they help you become more aligned. Don't you
find your mind is more peaceful when you're using something that
works well rather than struggling with something that doesn't? My
son has taught me a lot about quality. From a young boy, he's always
enjoyed high quality stuff. Technology, food, clothes, hotels and
even the restaurants where he dines. In the past, I used to encourage
him to have cheaper things to save myself money due to my own
stinginess! He appreciates quality so much that he'll even go without
things rather than make compromises, which I guess would be
compromising himself. I've benefitted a lot from my son's wisdom;
even when he was a young boy. You can learn a lot from children.

Obtaining things for pleasure

You may have asked yourself how The Process caters for obtaining things
purely for pleasure. You might eat a piece of cake just for pleasure, when
you don't actually need the sugar or calories. You might purchase a beautiful
car that's far more luxurious than you really need. Some spiritual teachers
tell you it's fine to have such things – so long as you don't become attached
to them. Other spiritual teachers might tell you that obtaining things for
pleasure is greedy.

What I've observed in myself and others, is that the more aligned you
become, the less pleasure and luxury you need. Ultimately, you'll be happy

enjoying the pleasure that's given to you as a bi-product of following The Guidelines. You won't need to seek out pleasure in the form of doing or obtaining certain things. And if pleasure is presented to you, you can enjoy it skillfully, without becoming attached.

Letting go of obtaining things for the sake of pleasure is a gradual process. If you end up *trying* to let go of acquiring pleasure before you're naturally ready to do so, it will cause harm rather than creating peace. Sustained suppression leads to unpleasant emotions and depression. Part of practicing The Guidelines is about being honest and kind to yourself.

> Gently work with the practices and invite yourself to need less pleasure.

Then, over time, the amount of pleasure you crave for and acquire reduces, whilst The Process continues to offer you just the right amount of pleasure, which you can enjoy without attachment. In the meantime, if you feel you need to obtain pleasurable things, or arrange pleasurable activities, then it's a matter of aligning them with The Guidelines as best you can.

What I've noticed myself is the type of pleasure I've craved for over the years has transformed. Craving for crude pleasures like luxurious foods, sex and material things has reduced. It's been substituted by craving more for refined pleasures, like the beauty of nature, studying spiritual books, and the pleasant feelings I experience in my body when I'm meditating.

Simplicity and spaciousness

There's an obvious relationship between the number of things you own and simplicity.

> In general, the fewer things you own, the simpler your life.

A simpler life means it's easier to cultivate being present. You don't need to think so much about all the things you have; managing them, using them, cleaning them, replacing them and so on. Have you ever let go of something that you didn't need that's been taking up a lot of time and energy? It's a relief! You experience pleasurable feelings when you let go of things you don't need. The Process rewards you for becoming more aligned.

Less stuff means more space. When your environments are cluttered it's harder to remain present. Orderly, spacious environments lend themselves to peace and concentration. A business I worked for had a wonderful office in London which I visited occasionally. As soon as I stepped through the door I felt more present and peaceful. It was as though something had mysteriously changed my state of mind. As a result of this, it was far easier to communicate well and concentrate on my work. Have you ever observed how your mindset changes when you're in orderly and spacious environments, in comparison with environments that are chaotic and cluttered? There's a link between an orderly environment and an orderly mind. There's also a link between a spacious environment and a spacious mind.

Spacious environments cultivate a peaceful mind because the space allows you to connect to the stillness within The Process. This is where the true peace and intelligence resides. Behind all of the form, all of the objects, people, and the rest of nature, is stillness or emptiness. It's like the blank canvas of a painting. You can access the intelligence from within The Process through this emptiness. Spacious locations and spacious views have the same effect. When you look out across an ocean, most of what you see is space. When you look at clouds in the sky, there's lots of space between you and clouds. Space you create in your environments through letting go of things you don't need, helps you to align with the guideline, "Be present, bringing awareness and acceptance into every moment."

Many religions and philosophies discuss this space. The Bhagavad Gita refers to it using the Sanskrit word 'akasha.' The subtlest of all elements that links form with the formless. The Process offers this space to link you to its infinite intelligence and become more skillful. I enjoy looking into space – I become peaceful and present. You can look into space from wherever you are. There's always space to look at. Even in a cluttered environment, there will be pockets of space between you and the stuff around you. Connecting with this subtle element, allows you to access true wisdom and the power of The Guidelines without any conscious thought, knowledge or memory recall. It's a powerful technique and access point. Listening to silence is another gateway that has the same effect.

)) Create a habit of staring into space, and listening to silence.

Keep the body very still, relaxed, and alert, as you do this. If you invite an open mind and heart, what you connect with is far more subtle and deeper than what you usually experience.

Greed

Greed is triggered by selfishness, and selfishness is a characteristic of the ego. Being selfish, requires us to believe we're separate to others. Conceptually we are separate, but the reality is that we're all one – all part of The Process. Greed and selfishness are based on delusion.

Greed is desiring more than you need. You don't necessarily need an excess amount of something to be greedy. Excessive longing for things causes greed. And that's regardless of whether you actually get what you long for. Greed isn't just about wealth or things. You can be greedy for anything including attention, success, fame, emotional pain or experiences. Desiring more spiritual progress in your lifetime than The Process has planned for you is also a form of greed – it causes stress.

The positive opposite to greed is generosity. Some people are so generous that they give up opportunities for their own spiritual development for the benefits of others – like giving away valuable spiritual books or letting go of attending a retreat to allow somebody else to take their place. This kind of altruistic behavior demonstrates a deep understanding that we're all connected and evolving together as one.

Obtaining luxurious items or services for the sake of pleasure, when there are alternatives of an adequate quality is greedy. Luxury is often used as a way of acquiring pleasure. Using pleasure to escape from pain creates addictions. Beliefs about having luxurious items, or consuming luxurious services, are created by the ego to add to the false sense of self. Believing you're better than somebody else because you own a more luxurious home is an example of this. I've had many thoughts like this; considering my material wealth to justify feeling 'better' than somebody else who has less. In the past, I've used this to artificially boost my low self-esteem.

What constitutes luxury is a matter of personal opinion, obligations and culture. I have a laptop that I deem to be of an adequate quality for what I need. I don't view it as being luxurious, but some people might regard it as a luxury. You have to feel your way around this guideline. When you're present you'll know whether the things you obtain are luxurious or not, given your context. Some spiritual teachers say that it's fine to have whatever you want, even luxury items, so long as you're mindful in the way that you acquire and use them. The Buddha taught that suffering is caused through our psychological attachments to things, rather than the things themselves.

Luxuries can separate people and groups. It makes it easier for those who are less spiritually evolved to adopt an 'us and them' mentality. It also feeds and reinforces egos in a positive and negative way. People can view themselves as being better or worse than others based on what they own or experience. I hope that future generations enjoy a more level playing field when it comes to possessions and experiences. Balance and equality across everybody would demonstrate kindness is being practiced on a grand scale.

Speaking from my own experience, I've enjoyed plenty of luxuries in the past, and continue to do so. I know that at times, I've used luxuries to prop me up, and make me feel better about myself. Purchasing luxurious products, driving luxurious cars, even drinking luxurious hot chocolates with cream and marshmallows!

As I mentioned before, most of us aren't evolved enough to live without all of our luxuries. The practice here is to observe yourself. And then to kindly withdraw luxuries only when you know it's not going to cause any real harm. Feeling depressed because you don't have your luxuries isn't following The Guidelines. Letting go of things is often a gradual process and it needs to feel natural.

> **Let go of your luxuries when you're ready and motivated to do so.**

One thing at a time. You have your whole lifetime to practice. The Process responds to greed with corrections. These take many forms including loss. You hear about people accumulating far more than they need and then ending up losing some or all of it. This can be due to all sorts of things like accidents, stock market crashes, theft or some other reason. Corrections are often channeled through people you come into contact with; people who threaten what you have or prevent you from getting more of it. When you experience this, it's The Process messaging you about greed. If somebody prevents you from acquiring more than you need, your ego may view that person as an enemy. The truth is that they're helping you – they're serving The Process and supporting your spiritual progress. Whether they're aware of it or not, they're taking the role of 'corrector.' The Process has arranged for them to take that role. You should be grateful to these people.

Connections with other guidelines

All seven guidelines connect together, and support each other. The table below highlights a few of the connections between "Harmoniously obtain and retain only what you need" and the other guidelines.

Guideline	Connections
Honor the body	• Obtain and retain what's needed to care for the body.
Be present, bringing awareness and acceptance into every moment	• Letting go of stuff you don't need leads to a simpler life. Simplicity helps you become more present. • The space you create in your environments through letting go of things you don't need will help align you with the guideline "Be present, bringing awareness and acceptance into every moment." • Make a habit of staring into space or listening to silence to help you become present.
Act with kindness, considering everyone and everything	• Giving away items you don't need is an act of generosity. • In the process of obtaining anything, be kind to yourself and others. • We should practice kindness to ourselves and others when we're letting go of items. • Only take things when somebody is comfortable giving them to you. • Be straightforward with people. Never use manipulative tactics to obtain things. • Be kind to yourself in the process of earning money to purchase things. • Be kind to others by earning money to pay for the things you need in an honest and straightforward way. • Obtain things that have been ethically produced or sourced. • The positive opposite of greed is generosity, which is a component of kindness.
Understand the truth, communicating it selectively and skillfully	• Be honest with yourself about what you really need to obtain and retain.
Do only what needs to be done	• The fewer items you own, the less activity is required to maintain them. • The fewer items you purchase, the less work may be required to earn money to pay for them. • Take responsibility for ensuring that you have quality items that enable you to do what needs to be done.
Apply The Guidelines to your digital device usage	• Let go of any digital items you don't need like files, apps and information stored on devices. • Only access digital content when there's a real need to.

You can find a list of ideas for practicing this guideline in the final chapter "Building & Structuring Your Practice."

POINTS FOR REFLECTION

1. The Process knows exactly what items you need to live harmoniously at any given time.

2. Let go of what you don't need. Retain what you already have and need. Harmoniously obtain what you need, but don't have.

3. Reviewing your items regularly, maybe once per quarter, will help you become more aligned.

4. We should kindly consider ourselves and others when letting go of items.

5. If you get your needs met you'll be peaceful. If you don't get what you need, you'll suffer.

6. You need items to ensure that you can meet obligations to yourself and others.

7. The more aligned you become, the less pleasure and luxury you desire.

8. Letting go of obtaining things for the sake of pleasure is a gradual process.

9. You experience pleasurable feelings when you let go of things you don't need.

10. There's a link between an orderly environment and an orderly mind. There's also a link between a spacious environment and a spacious mind.

11. Doing without luxuries and then feeling depressed isn't following The Guidelines.

12. Letting go of things is often a gradual process and needs to feel natural.

Apply The Guidelines to Your Digital Device Usage

Stated negatively: Do not disregard The Guidelines in your digital device usage

THE PROCESS HAS CREATED the Internet-enabled digital device era. I'm referring to things like phones, computers, tablets, TVs, virtual reality headsets and smart watches. The speed at which digital device usage has spread is phenomenal. Many of us are spending hours of our time each day using these devices – usually looking at screens. There's an exponentially increasing number of digitally enabled processes within The Process. From ordering products online, to paying a bill in a restaurant or organizing a meeting with friends.

Guideline: Apply The Guidelines to Your Digital Device Usage

We're following digital processes when we're communicating through messaging and other online channels. More and more processes are becoming digitized. The reason why some people are resistant and suffering, is that they don't know how to use their devices consciously. When you align yourself with The Guidelines and use digital devices consciously, you can be at peace with them and enjoy their benefits.

Through contemplating the other guidelines, you can make connections to how digital device usage applies. For example, ensuring a good posture when using a computer is honoring the body. Using social media only when you really need to, is doing only what needs to be done. If people practiced all the other guidelines perfectly, there would be no need to consider digital device usage as a separate guideline. However, because of the exponential rise in digital device usage, and a growing number of device addictions and problems, it felt right for me to address digital device usage directly and highlight it as a key area of practice for everybody.

When I was considering this guideline, I soon realized there are enough pointers to fill a book dedicated to digital device usage. I produced a shorter, high-level list of principles that encompass all of the detailed guidance. These are called 'The Seven Principles of Conscious Digital Device Usage.' If you follow these, you'll align your digital device usage with what The Process needs. Practicing these principles will help humanity evolve through the digital era, as well as allowing you to live a life of harmony today.

The Seven Principles of Conscious Digital Device Usage
1. Only use a device when it's really needed
2. Stay mindful during device usage
3. Be kind to your body during device usage
4. Communicate selectively, truthfully and skillfully during device usage
5. Have time away from your devices every day
6. Take opportunities for real human contact
7. Accept that digital device usage is part of life

Only use a device when it's really needed

Digital device usage is aligned when it's responding to a real need. Here are some examples:

- You're lost somewhere and need to use your phone to find directions.
- You check your computer for an important email you're expecting.
- You look at your phone to see who's calling before deciding whether to answer.
- You use your computer to do your work.
- You share something on social media that you know people will need.

These are examples of what I call *conscious usage*; you respond to a need. Unconscious usage, on the other hand, is when you use the device reactively without a real need. Some examples of this are:

- You feel lonely, so you reach for your phone without even thinking about it, and log onto social media.
- You enter a queue at a retail outlet. You automatically look at your phone without consciously deciding to do so.
- You're working on your computer and concentrating on an important task. A notification pops up for an email that can be responded to later. You read the email straight away and interrupt the task you needed to get done.
- You're missing your ex-partner. You look at their social media feed, and check out who they've been dating even although you know it upsets you.

Without making a conscious decision, many people's minds are programmed to reach for their device, switch it on, and hunt for stimulus. Because much of the content is personalized and supports people's identifications, their egos love it! When we're not present during usage, the ego uses the content to reinforce its identifications. It also makes comparisons with others to enhance its false sense of self and separateness.

Using a device as an escape from the present moment, usually to avoid unpleasant feelings, is also a form of unconscious usage. It's a form of addiction. The ego is using the device to escape from something that's unpleasant. It's similar to when a smoker lights a cigarette if they're feeling emotional. The first truth about unconscious usage is that it takes people away from life. It takes them away from the present moment, and into a dream about the past or future. This is something we're just beginning to realize. When useful things like smart phones get introduced to the masses, they get used inappropriately and turn into a global addiction. The second truth about unconscious usage and any addiction, is that it prevents people from facing unpleasant feelings and healing emotional pain. The only way to heal is to be present with your feelings.

I created and use a technique called *Stop! – Check – Use*. It helps me check that I'm only using my devices when I really need to. It involves creating a habit of stopping every time you experience a desire to use a device: *Stop!* Then take a second or two to check you really 'need' to use it: *Check*. You can then make a conscious decision as to whether you should then *Use* the device, or *Let go* of using it at that moment in time. It's a quick technique to apply and after using it a few times, over a few days, you'll create a habit.

> Make it second nature to *Stop! – Check – Use.*

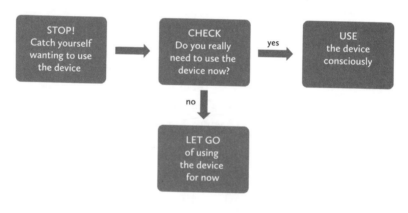

Stop! – Check – Use

Stay mindful during device usage

This second principle should be applied you when you've made a conscious decision to use the device. If you've applied *Stop! – Check – Use* or a similar technique, you'll already be mindful when you begin use. Being mindful, or being present, is about being aware and accepting of your experience. There are three big factors that influence your ability to stay mindful during usage. The first is how mindful you are before you start using the device. The second is how you respond or react to the content that's presented to you. And the third is how simple the device is to use. Here are twelve tips to help you stay mindful during digital device usage:

1 **Only access content and enable notifications that are really needed**

When you're accessing content that you really need, you'll be better placed to stay mindful. If you access content that you don't need, it's highly likely that you'll get lost in thoughts and emotions. Consciously decide what content you're going to access on your device. Also, take responsibility for notifications and alerts. Only configure notifications and real time updates that you definitely need. Otherwise, let go of the distractions and choose when you access things. The more unnecessary notifications you react to, the less you'll be in control of your state of mind when you access their content. Unnecessary notifications distract you from other activities that require your full attention.

2 **Avoid content you know will trigger negative reactions**

If there's content that you know is going to push your buttons, triggering you to become lost in your thoughts and emotions, avoid it. Otherwise, you're harming yourself. You wouldn't put your hand in a fire. In the same way, don't compromise your energy or alignment by exposing yourself to difficult content. This might mean avoiding certain websites, TV shows, or social media feeds. I'll often mute social media feeds from people my ego finds difficult rather than disconnecting from them altogether. It keeps communication open, with the option of re-engaging later, as and when it's more appropriate to do so.

3 **If possible, ensure you use good quality digital devices**

This is especially true if you spend a lot of time on them. It's going to be much easier to stay mindful if you're working on a device that's fast and simple to use. Rather than one that's sluggish and complex. When technology appears to be working against you, it's even more challenging to stay mindful.

4 **Configure your devices to make them easier to use**

There's a correlation between simplicity and being mindful. There's lots you can do to simplify devices, including removing unwanted apps and freeing up space to help make the device go faster. Even detail such as configuring menus and shortcuts that suit your usage will simplify things. If you don't know how then ask somebody technical for support. A friend or store assistant might be able to help.

5   **Keep some awareness on your breath or bodily sensations**

This is a de facto technique used to become mindful and retain mindfulness.

6   **Be aware of thoughts and feelings**

If you're able to, observe your thoughts and feelings whilst using devices. This will keep you aware and present. If you catch your thoughts turning negative or experience unpleasant feelings, stop using the device for a moment. Review what you're experiencing or communicating.

7   **Monitor internal resistance**

If you catch yourself in a state of resistance as you use your device, then something needs to change. Internal resistance indicates misalignment. You either need to bring acceptance to your experience with whatever content you're involved in or avoid the content. Internal resistance can also manifest when the body's uncomfortable or you need a break from usage.

8   **Be aware of the space between you and the screen**

For devices with screens, there's space between your eyes and the screen. Be aware of that space at the same time as you're looking at the screen. This will protect your mind from getting lost in the content. Awareness of space helps you stay mindful. The space also acts as a gateway for you to access the intelligence within The Process.

9   **Take breaks from using your device**

Briefly look away from your screen every few minutes. Rest your eyes or look at something else in your physical environment. Something natural like a plant or the sky if possible. Every twenty minutes or so, have a break to do something physical. Even if it's a quick stand or stretch. This will refresh you and keep you alert. It's far more challenging to stay mindful when you're tired.

10 **Change your device's aesthetics**

Change your background or screen saver now and again; or rearrange icons in a way that's optimized for your current usage. This will keep your digital experience fresh. Changes in what we see and experience helps us to stay mindful.

11 **Be kind to your body during device usage**

When the body's comfortable it's easier to stay mindful – more on this in the next section.

12 **Communicate selectively, truthfully, and skillfully during usage**

Skillful communication and mindfulness go together. When you're communicating skillfully, you're mindful. And when you're mindful, you communicate skillfully. The asynchronous nature of messaging can help us to communicate more mindfully. Messaging allows us to pause for longer than we might during communication in person or over the phone. Before reading or sending a message, you may observe a brief pause, and use that to check that you're present. Whatever communication follows immediately from that will be aligned.

Be kind to your body during device usage

When you are kind to your body during device usage, it feels good. It's also far more likely that you'll use your device consciously. It's much easier to be mindful and skillful when your body is settled. Maintaining a good posture during device usage helps your energy flow freely, leading to better awareness and concentration. Ideally, during usage, maintain a posture that's both relaxed and alert. This will have a balancing effect on the mind.

There's plenty of practical advice available that covers looking after your body whilst using devices like computers and phones. The advice changes over time as we learn more. Take time out occasionally to research the current recommendations. Review how you're using your devices. For example, check your posture. Monitor yourself to ensure you take regular screen breaks. If you're using devices at your place of work, you can find out if the organization has health and safety guidance you can follow.

Being kind to your body is also about keeping yourself safe.

> **Devices should only be used when it's safe to do so.**

Many people use devices unsafely and believe they're free from the consequences. There are always consequences in being unsafe. Even if the mind doesn't understand that device usage is risky, the body will still create stress as the body is intelligent enough to know when you're unsafe. When you are using your device in a dangerous situation it is highly likely that you are lost in thought at the time. This means that your usage will be unskillful and harmful. A prime example of this is somebody crossing a busy road whilst messaging on their phone. Assuming they get to the other side uninjured and alive, their bodies will have created some stress as intuitively they'd know they were taking a risk. And other people in the vicinity may also have felt stressed through observing them. It really does make sense to use your devices only when it's safe to do so.

Communicate selectively, truthfully and skillfully during device usage

This principle is about applying the guideline, "Understand the truth, communicating it selectively and skillfully" to your device usage. To help with this, I'll use some pointers introduced in Chapter Six and provide examples of how they're relevant to digital communication. Digital communication is more than just communicating directly with other people. It also encompasses how you communicate with websites, including the information you provide on entry forms and posts to forums.

- **Communicating Kindly** – It may help you to keep in mind the three components of kindness when communicating with people: Consideration, friendliness and generosity. With digital communication you can be connecting with masses of people in a short period of time. This can be the case with social media usage. In some situations, it's kindest to be brief and transactional if you know people are busy. Sometimes, being considerate means not being outwardly considerate. Being friendly means not being outwardly friendly. And being generous means not being outwardly generous. It's really a matter of tuning into the person or group you're communicating with. And then deciding what communication is best for you all. The simple act of being considerate to who you're communicating with is enough. Regardless of the results. With written communication, keep in mind that people read things differently. Part of being kind is to communicate in a way that's clear and straightforward.

- **Communicating Usefully** – We have the opportunity to communicate and be heard as much as we wish in the digital era. It takes energy to communicate, and energy to process what's communicated to you. This applies to any channel including telephone calls, messaging, emails or social media. When you're communicating usefully, your communication is aligned with The Guidelines. It's the type of communication The Process appreciates. If you have the opportunity, observe a brief pause before communicating anything. Ask yourself if it's needed and useful. If you know you're communicating content to people who don't need it, you're wasting their time and energy. It's a form of stealing. By filtering your communication in this way, what you do communicate will be more impactful and helpful. If you already know that you're the kind of person who communicates excessively, work with the mantra "less is more."

- **Harmonious Communication** – In the chapter on communication, I encourage harmonious communication, rather than divisive communication. This is particularly important with written communication through devices. Everything you communicate leaves a trace. It may be stored in various places for your whole life or longer. With social media, what you communicate can be accessed by millions of people. The impact of your written communication via devices is significant. When you communicate harmoniously, you bring people together and encourage kindness. It's a wonderful contribution to make online and encourages others to do the same.

- **Conscious Sharing of Information** – You can share information directly or indirectly whilst being online. This might be about yourself, other people or situations. Direct sharing is when you directly share facts like where you are, what you've been doing, or how you're feeling. Indirect sharing is when you share information that somebody can use to infer other things. For example, if you're sharing information about being with a particular friend, and they're sharing information about their location, your location can be inferred. There's also the practical matter about maintaining your privacy online for security and safety reasons. It's not for me to tell you what you should or shouldn't share. That's your decision. However, I would like to encourage you to share consciously. Take a moment to think about the potential impact to yourself and others before disclosing information.

- **Slow down** – especially if you tend to communicate at breakneck speed. This will help you stay present.

- **Be conscious of your current state of mind** – check in with your mood and feelings. If you're at peace with yourself, it will be far easier to communicate skillfully. Be careful about communicating when you're experiencing unpleasant feelings like stress, anxiety or fear. In these instances, you may even choose to communicate later; at a time when you're feeling more settled.

- **Pause briefly, before communicating online** – ask yourself these four questions about what you plan to share:
  a. Is it kind?
  b. Is it useful?
  c. It is harmonious?
  d. Should I really be sharing that?

Have time away from your devices every day

Only you can determine how much time you spend on your devices. It's a personal thing, and depends very much on your own circumstances. What I know for sure, is that everybody needs time away from their devices. We have basic things to take care of to ensure our well-being. We need to look after our bodies, and give our eyes a break. We need proper relaxation and sleep. We need to engage with nature. We need real human contact. All of these things require time away from devices. My recommendation is to regularly review how much time you're spending using your devices. Be honest with yourself about whether you need to make changes.

Take opportunities for real human contact

Digital communication is now the primary way of connecting with people. Usually via messaging or social media. As useful as it is, it's no substitute for real human contact.

When I was writing this book, I had to wait a while before I was able to articulate why real human contact was so important. I knew it was needed, but couldn't explain why. I discussed the subject with an acquaintance, and after a few minutes, the light bulb lit up! She shared some of her own insights, I reflected on them, and then I realized why real human contact was so important...

When you are with people physically, it helps you grasp the fact that we're all connected and a part of The Process. It's easier to acknowledge the cause and effect between us. All of our actions have an impact. We're not really separate. Directly, or indirectly, we are all influencing each other. Everything we do has a ripple effect out to the rest of the universe. I appreciate you experience this whilst interacting digitally, but real human contact enables a much deeper, richer experience of this phenomenon.

When we're physically in the company of others, all the different aspects of experience are interacting. All of the senses may be used within the communication. We sometimes appreciate the important dimension of touch when we are with people physically. Whether it's a hug, a tap on the shoulder, a dance, or something more intimate like sex, it all helps with this realization.

If you're very receptive you'll notice energy passing between yourself and other people. It's difficult to explain this energy, as it's not form-based. You can't see it, hear it, smell it, taste it or touch it. I cannot explain how to experience it. I just know it's there. Your ability to experience this energy is influenced by awareness and a subtler connection with The Process. The experience isn't created through any of the five senses. It's experienced through another formless sense that cannot be explained.

Have you ever sensed that somebody is close to you when you haven't seen or heard them arrive? Or experienced energy from somebody who is angry without any factual evidence to confirm that's the case? These are examples of experiencing the energy I'm referring to. It takes many forms. Kind people transmit a warm and positive energy. Although you can sense energy without being with people physically, it's more prominent when you're actually with people.

Because there's more energy flowing during real human contact, communication is deeper. This leads to you understanding people better, making stronger connections and building closer relationships. The same applies in business. In general, you build closer relationships and work more effectively with people when you're together in person.

The real spiritual benefit of experiencing this energy, is that it helps you gain insights into The Process and how it operates. This energy binds The Process together. Down at an atomic level, it's the energy that exists between particles, providing connectivity and movement. It's beautiful; peaceful and still. How intriguing that peace and stillness can subtly move things around and create a range of experience for us. How it operates is a mystery. This energy may also be called love. Not romantic love that's dependent upon things; but pure and unconditional love. Be grateful for any real human contact you experience regardless of who it's with or how it feels. It's a gift – a wonderful way of deepening your knowing of The Process and what connects us all together as one.

Accepting that digital device usage is a part of life

For the vast majority of us, the use of digital devices including phones and computers is essential. More and more services like banking and shopping are becoming exclusively available via digital channels. In the future, I believe that it will be virtually impossible to get by in life without the use of digital devices.

I know people who resist digital devices. They believe they should be able to do everything via traditional non-digital means. Other people resist digital devices because they believe that using them is compromising their experience in one way or another. I'm sure this is true in some cases and everybody's entitled to their opinions. Opinions are harmless when you don't identify with them. However, resisting is what causes harm. Expecting the world to be less digital than it is now is like trying to turn back time and change things. It's impossible. It's draining when you crave for things now to be different to how they are now.

The upshot to all of this is that we need to accept and embrace digital devices. The way we engage with them is going to influence future generations. We have quite a responsibility. I'm hoping that we can enjoy all the positive benefits, live with the shortcomings and take responsibility for using them consciously. This is by far the best approach if we wish to live a life of harmony.

Connections with other guidelines

All seven guidelines connect together, and support each other. The table on the following page highlights a few of the connections between "Apply The Guidelines to your digital device usage" and the other guidelines.

Guideline	Connections
Honor the body	• Consider the impact of digital device usage on the body, and make necessary adjustments. • Maintaining a good posture during device usage allows energy to flow more freely in the body, leading to better concentration. • Have enough time away from your devices each day to allow yourself to relax the mind. • Use digital information, products and services to help you honor your body. • Take opportunities for real human contact when you can be with people physically. Your body needs this.
Be present, bringing awareness and acceptance into every moment	• Bring awareness and acceptance into your experience during device usage. • Monitor internal resistance during device usage. • Let go of accessing digital content that triggers stress and resistance. • Be aware of the space between you and the screen. • Keep some awareness on your breath or bodily sensations. • Briefly look away from your screen every few minutes. • Take regular breaks from using your devices. • Change your device's aesthetics. Replace your background or screen saver occasionally. • Stay aware of thoughts and feelings during device usage. • Accept that digital device usage is part of life.
Act with kindness, considering everyone and everything	• Use digital devices as vehicles for kindness. • Communicate kindly with your devices. • Avoid content that you know causes negative reactions. • Having sufficient time away from your devices each day is an act of kindness to your body and mind.
Understand the truth, communicating it selectively and skillfully	• Access digital content from sources you believe are likely to be truthful. • Let go of accessing digital content you believe is likely to be false. • Be selective about how much you communicate using digital means. • Be selective about whom you communicate with. • Communicate kindly, usefully and harmoniously whilst online. • Disclose information selectively and skillfully. • Try pausing briefly before communicating online and ask yourself these four questions about what you plan to share: a.Is it kind? b.Is it useful? c.Is it harmonious? d.Should I really be sharing that?
Do only what needs to be done	• Include your various digital activities within activity reviews. Especially those that are big time and energy consumers. • Review the amount of time you're spending on social media. • Only use a device when it's really needed. • Only access content and enable notifications that are really needed. • Practice the 'Stop! - Check – Use' technique.

Guideline	Connections
Harmoniously obtain and retain only what you need	• Let go of any digital items you don't need like files, apps and information stored on your devices. • Only access digital content when there's a real need. • If it's possible, ensure you have good quality digital devices.

You can find a list of ideas for practicing this guideline in the final chapter "Building & Structuring Your Practice."

POINTS FOR REFLECTION

1. The Seven Principles of Conscious Digital Device Usage:
   a. Only use a device when it's really needed.
   b. Stay mindful during device usage.
   c. Be kind to your body during device usage.
   d. Communicate selectively, truthfully and skillfully during device usage.
   e. Have time away from your devices every day.
   f. Take opportunities for real human contact.
   g. Accept that digital device usage is part of life.
2. Digital device usage is aligned when it's responding to a real need.
3. When we're not present during usage, the ego may use digital content to reinforce its identifications and make judgmental comparisons.
4. Using a device to avoid being with unpleasant emotions is a form of unconscious usage. It's also a form of addiction.
5. Make it second nature to *Stop! – Check – Use.*
6. When you're kind to your body during device usage it feels good. It's also more likely that you'll use your device consciously.
7. When you're using your device in a dangerous situation it's highly likely that you're lost in thought. This means your usage will be unskillful and harmful.
8. Communicate harmoniously with your devices.
9. Share information consciously with your devices.
10. Everybody needs time away from their devices.
11. As useful as it is, digital communication is no substitute for real human contact.
12. When you're with people physically it helps you grasp the fact that we're all connected and a part of The Process.

Chapter Ten

Building & Structuring
Your Practice

OVER THE LAST FEW CHAPTERS I've introduced you to The Process and The Guidelines. As I'm sure you'll appreciate, there's only so much that I can explain within a single book. The best way to deepen your understanding of The Process and master The Guidelines, is through practice. This final chapter is dedicated to helping you build a practice that's right for you at this point in time.

> Tread your own path and respect that everybody's practice and progress is different.

The Guidelines

173

Change and impermanence makes applying The Guidelines a real-time, lifelong practice. The structure of your practice will need reviewing and changing as your conditions change. I recommend that you undertake a practice review every month or quarter. In addition, a practice review may be helpful when major life circumstances change like your health, a personal relationship or your work situation.

People evolve and learn, even without a formal spiritual practice. Those who don't access spiritual teachings can still learn about The Guidelines through their own life experience. It's an effective way of learning and progressing. The downside is that it involves suffering. We make mistakes, the Process corrects us, we suffer, and hopefully we learn. Personally, I opt for studying and applying spiritual teachings. I enjoy more peace and happiness that way. When you find spiritual teachings that resonate, they're enjoyable to study and practice. To live a life of harmony, your practice needs to revolve around The Guidelines. Here's a reminder of them…

Guideline stated positively	Guideline stated negatively
Honor the body	Do not harm the body
Be present, bringing awareness and acceptance into every moment	Do not become lost in thought
Act with kindness, considering everyone and everything	Do not be intentionally harmful or single-minded in your actions
Understand the truth, communicating it selectively and skillfully	Avoid excessive, harmful and false communication
Do only what needs to be done	Do not do what is unnecessary
Harmoniously obtain and retain only what you need	Do not obtain or retain more than you need
Apply The Guidelines to your digital device usage	Do not disregard The Guidelines in your digital device usage

The Guidelines Stated Positively and Negatively

Benefits and measures

Here are four of many personal benefits you can enjoy when you follow The Guidelines, which I'm hoping will incentivize you to practice:

- **A peaceful mind** – There's a direct correlation between following The Guidelines and a peaceful mind. This means you spend less of your time lost in thoughts and emotions; and more time living in the present moment.

- **True enjoyment** – You can only truly enjoy things with a peaceful mind. Through being in the moment, being aware, and experiencing life now. I'm not referring to you 'enjoying' yourself through intoxication or fantasy. I'm referring to *true enjoyment*. The best enjoyment there is. Enjoyment of life in the present moment.

- **Less suffering** – The Process corrects you for disregarding The Guidelines. Corrections always involve suffering. It's both necessary and unpleasant! Fortunately, when you follow The Guidelines, you suffer less.

- **Better relationships** – Following The Guidelines means being at peace with what is, what's been and what's to come. This frees you from tension within relationships and promotes harmony. As a result of this, the majority of your interactions with people will be positive and harmonious.

Interestingly, these benefits are also measures. You can use them to gauge the progress you're making. When your mind becomes more peaceful you suffer less, relationships improve and you enjoy life more. You know you're on the right track. Through practicing, you're likely to enjoy quick wins that motivate you. That said, it's best to measure your progress over longer periods of time. The four measures fluctuate over time based on your life conditions. It's similar to looking at a graph that's showing a successful stock market investment. It may fluctuate in the short term, but over a longer period of time you'll see an upward trend as the value of your investments increase.

You may recall from Chapter Four that your experience of dreams is a good measure of progress. If you start recollecting dreams more, knowing when you're dreaming, and consciously following The Guidelines within dreams, you're heading in the right direction. The benefits and measures apply as much to dreams as they do to your waking life.

Three areas of practice

There are three areas of practice needed to align yourself. I've illustrated these in the diagram on the next page. The first is through structured practices like meditation, yoga, journaling or study. The second area is applying The Guidelines in your everyday activities. Being kind in your communication to others is an example of this. The third area is your life conditions.

Configuring your life so that it's conducive to following The Guidelines. An example of this is letting go of a dysfunctional relationship or taking up regular exercise. To have a rounded practice and to make progress, all three areas need to be addressed. I advise you to keep these areas in mind as you review your practice on a regular basis.

Three Areas of Practice

Neglecting your practice in one area will compromise your ability to align via the other two. For example, if your life conditions are set up so that you work in a toxic and harmful environment, it'll be very difficult to make progress with meditation or have a clear mind for study. And the positive opposite applies. For example, if you work in a peaceful and kind environment, it will help you make more progress in areas such as meditation and applying The Guidelines in your everyday activities.

> Always keep the three areas in mind when you're reviewing your practice.

The opportunities for practice in the next section provide examples across all areas.

Opportunities for practice

The table on the following page provides a few ideas you can incorporate into your practice. The first section offers some general practices, followed by options for each of The Guidelines.

> Have a look through the table, review the chapters, be creative, and then decide what practices you'd like to work with at this point in time.

Less is usually more. You may be able to find new opportunities that combine a number of practice areas. For example, starting a yoga practice helps you work on honoring the body and being present. Whatever your lifestyle, there will always be opportunities to apply The Guidelines. To begin with, I recommend you focus on up to three practices at any one time. A balance of easier and more challenging practices works well.

General Practices

- **Daily Gratitude** – Take a couple of minutes each day to reflect on all of the things you've appreciated. Even the small things. Be grateful to The Process for providing those experiences.

- **Daily Corrections Reflection** – Take five minutes each day to consider times when you've suffered. If possible, determine the cause of the suffering including the guidelines that were being disregarded.

- **Guidelines Reminder** – Take a couple of minutes each day to review the list of guidelines. This will help keep them front of mind. Look for creative opportunities to recite them. For example, in yoga practice, you can mentally recite a new guideline every time you change posture. Other options are to recite The Guidelines whilst taking a walk or during meditation.

- **Spiritual Friendship** – If you have friends who are aware of The Guidelines, make time to explore and discuss them together.

- **Study** – Allocate a regular time slot to study. Re-read the chapters of this book, and other quality spiritual texts, that help you become aligned. Sign up to my email newsletter and social media feeds for regular teachings through **www.darrencockburn.com**.

- **The Process Reflections** – It's helpful to keep The Process in mind whenever you can. By doing this you return to the present moment and become mindful. It gives you perspective. Allocate regular time slots to reflect on The Process and try the reflection techniques in Chapter One.

- **Reflective Writing and Journaling** – Some people find writing about The Process and The Guidelines a great way of reflecting on the teachings. You might want to write blog entries, publish snippets on social media or write in a personal journal.

- **Teachers & Coaching** – Spend time with somebody who can help you understand and apply The Guidelines. This is particularly helpful if you're practicing alone. I offer coaching in this area. Details can be found at **www.darrencockburn.com**.

- **Start a Practice Group** – Find people in your local area or online who are also working with The Guidelines. Create a practice group. Arrange to meet regularly in person or through online group video calls. I sometimes offer access to these groups through my website **www.darrencockburn.com**.

- **Sequencing** – Create a sequence of practices aligned with The Guidelines; then execute them in a pre-determined order. For example, you might have a routine where you honor your body by doing some yoga, cultivate being present through meditation, and then do what needs to be done in your home. That would apply three guidelines in sequence. Sequencing installs helpful routines and habits. Create sequences that work for you and apply them on a regular basis.

- **Relationships** – Review your relationships, considering how they might help or hinder alignment based on the seven guidelines. Carefully consider whether you need to change or let go of certain relationships. Be grateful for the relationships that are helping you become more aligned.

- **Practice Reviews** – Undertake a regular practice review every month or quarter. A practice review is also helpful when major life circumstances change like your health, a personal relationship or your work situation.

Honor the body (Chapter Three)

- Wherever possible, place the genuine needs of the body first, above everything else.

- Ensure you're eating, sleeping, resting and exercising well.

- Keep your diet balanced with food and drink containing carbohydrates, healthy fats, proteins, vitamins, minerals, fiber and water.

- If your body experiences problems, find out whether diet is contributing in some way and make any necessary adjustments.

- Balance the amount of food and drink you consume to positively influence your energy levels.

- Integrate planned and spontaneous relaxation into your day.

- Practice Yoga Nidra to relax the body and mind. Integrate an intention into the practice based on The Guidelines.

- Review and implement some of the sleep tips found in Chapter Three.

- Review the latest physical activity advice from a trusted source. Make any changes required.

- Feel energy in the body by bringing some awareness to your hands or feet.

- Keep a journal for a few days to help raise awareness of energy levels. Log whether your energy has been low, balanced or excessively high. Reviewing events leading up to the log entry will help you understand what you may need to change to balance your energy.

Be present, bringing awareness and acceptance into every moment (Chapter Four)

- Explore mindfulness teachings outside of what you find in this book to help you become more aligned.

- Observe the two modes of the mind - being present or lost in thought.

- Ask yourself, "Am I present?" When you ask yourself this question you automatically become present.

- Reflect on what it's like to be lost in thought. When was the last time this happened to you and how did it negatively impact things? Then take another moment to reflect on what it's like to be present. When was the last time this happened to you and how did it positively impact things?

- When you're lost in unhelpful thought patterns and can't seem to pull yourself back into a mindful state, try doing something physical like taking a walk. That in itself, can be enough to help you become mindful and peaceful again.

- The next time you're experiencing unpleasant emotions, if the conditions allow you to, bring full awareness to them. Focus on them fully. Allow yourself to feel the unpleasantness within your body. Accept your feelings and use the moment as a positive opportunity to heal.

- Use the four ways of positively working with emotional pain:

  - Bring awareness and acceptance to feelings.

  - Change your physical state.

  - Change your conditions to minimize the chances of the feelings being triggered in the future.

  - Seek help from a wise friend or therapist.

- Carry out some analysis to determine your identifications. Your identifications are what cause you to become lost in thought.

- If you find yourself lost in thought, reflect on what you've been thinking and determine which of your identifications were active at the time.

- Sit or stand comfortably without concentrating on anything in particular. Bring awareness to the different components of your experience: bodily sensations, things coming in through the senses, feelings and thoughts.

- Raise your awareness through meditation by systematically cycling around the different aspects of your experience. Starting with your bodily sensations, moving onto things coming in through the senses, followed by your feelings and then your thoughts.

- Maintain some awareness on your breath to keep yourself grounded when involved in activities including listening to others.

- Practice a breathing meditation.

- Practice Yoga Nidra to increase your awareness and relax the whole body.

- Establish a physical yoga practice. Use it to increase body awareness, whilst helping build strength and flexibility.

- If possible, work on maintaining a straight posture. Not just within meditation, but whenever you need to stay aware.

- Allow your awareness to become an intoxication detective! Spot the times when your mind is becoming, or has been intoxicated, and then reflect on what needs to change to help you stay grounded in the future.

- Identify your own triggers for intoxication. Take steps to ensure that you reduce the likelihood of becoming intoxicated. Either take yourself away from the triggers or increase the intensity of your awareness when you know you might be at risk.

- If you're at a stage where you can be present on demand, instruct yourself to become present just before sleep. Alternatively, observe the breath or practice body awareness for a few minutes before sleep.

Act with kindness, considering everyone and everything (Chapter Five)

- Try mindful cleaning. Give the whole experience your full attention.

- When you experience common themes of resistance that keep repeating, preventing you from being peaceful and kind, investigate them. This may mean getting help from a wise friend or therapist.

- Practice generosity by being present in somebody's company and mindfully listening to them.

- Be generous to nature by enjoying it. This gives nature the opportunity to be appreciated and express its gratitude for being.

- Practice loving kindness meditation (also known as Metta Bhavana). This is a formal meditation practice that involves bringing to mind yourself, people to whom you can express kindness to easily, people you have problems with, strangers and everybody else in the world.

- Do only what needs to be done. By following this guideline, which is detailed in Chapter Seven, we end up needing to do less for ourselves. We let go of spending time doing stuff that isn't helpful. The time that's freed up can then be used for the kind service of others.

- Be around kind people. Kindness is propagated by people. Everything else being equal, if you're around people who are kind, you'll cultivate more kindness.

- Take opportunities to be kind. There will be many times when acts of kindness enter your consciousness. Follow up on them.

- Accept kindness from others – it's generous to the person who is being kind to you; plus you're acknowledging that they're following The Guidelines.

- Create a habit of staring into space, or listening to silence. Keep the body very still, relaxed and alert as you do this. If you invite an open mind and heart, what you connect with will be infinitely more subtle and deeper than what you usually experience.

Understand the truth, communicating it selectively and skillfully (Chapter Six)

- Check what you're believing is true by validating it against (i) direct perception (ii) inference or (iii) a trusted source.

- Practice being selective in your communication. Only communicate what you need to.

- If you tend to rush your communication, make a conscious effort to pause before speaking. Ask yourself whether what you plan to communicate is really necessary and helpful.

- Pay careful attention to everything you communicate.

- Practice true listening by following the guideline, "Be present, bringing awareness and acceptance into every moment" as you listen to others. You can use true listening as a mindfulness practice.

- Practice skillful self-disclosure.

- If you're sharing opinions with others rather than facts, you should communicate them as such. Caveating opinions as opinions is communicating truthfully.

- In challenging situations or when you're feeling at risk of saying something unskillful, slow down. You're always best to say something slowly and skillfully, rather than fast and unskillfully.

Do only what needs to be done (Chapter Seven)

- Doing only what needs to be done involves aligning your activities with The Guidelines. To do this, review your existing activities using the approach in Chapter Seven.

- Take responsibility for doing things to meet your needs. This is a form of kindness. Dedicate such action to others. Taking care of yourself puts you in a better position to serve others.

- Identify and work towards releasing your addictions. This helps you let go of doing things you don't need to do.

- If you work, regularly check to see that your job is aligned by using the pointers in Chapter Seven.

Harmoniously obtain and retain only what you need (Chapter Eight)

- To align with this guideline, apply these three simple rules:
    1. *Let go* of what you don't need.
    2. *Retain* what you already have and do need.
    3. *Harmoniously obtain* what you don't have, and do need.
- Review your items regularly to help you become more aligned.
- Only take things when somebody is comfortable giving them to you.
- Only obtain what you can genuinely afford.
- Be kind to yourself and others in the process of earning money.
- Obtain things that have been ethically produced or sourced.
- Go for quality; items created mindfully and ethically. These are the ideal things to source.
- Adjust your environments so they are spacious and orderly. This makes it easier to cultivate being present.
- Let go of your luxuries when you're ready and motivated to do so.

Apply The Guidelines to your digital device usage (Chapter Nine)

- Only use your device when it's really needed.
- Practice the *Stop! – Check – Use* technique.

- Stay mindful during device usage.
  - Keep some awareness on your breath or bodily sensations during device usage.
  - Be aware of thoughts and feelings during device usage.
- Monitor your internal resistance during device usage.
- Be aware of the space between you and the screen during device usage.
- Be kind to your body during device usage.
- Take time out occasionally to research recommendations on looking after your body whilst using devices like computers and phones.
- Communicate selectively, truthfully and skillfully during device usage.
- Have time away from your devices every day.
- Take opportunities for real human contact.
- Only access content and enable notifications that are really needed.
- Avoid content that you know will trigger negative reactions.
- If possible, ensure you use good quality digital devices.
- Configure your devices to make them easier to use.
- Take regular breaks when you are working with your devices.
- Change your devices' aesthetics like your wallpaper or screensaver.
- Work to ensure your digital communication is kind, useful and harmonious.
- Before you communicate online:
  - If needs be, slow down.
  - Be conscious of your current state of mind and emotions.
  - Pause briefly.
- Then ask yourself these four questions about what you plan to share:
  - Is it kind?
  - Is it useful?
  - It is harmonious?
  - Should I really be sharing that?
- Regularly review how much time you're spending using your devices and ensure you take time away from them.

General challenges and questions

Here are some general challenges, and frequently asked questions, people may ask when they're practicing The Guidelines. I've included my response to each of them.

- **"I'm not making any progress"** – Progress is made at different rates across different timeframes. Practice patience and acceptance. If you measure your progress over a longer period of time, you'll probably find that you're doing better than you might think.

- **"How will I ever perfect this?"** – Perfecting The Guidelines is the vision. For most people, it takes several lifetimes to perfect The Guidelines. Go for progress, not perfection. Be grateful that you can take steps in the right direction.

- **"Why is my friend better at following a guideline than me?"** – Everybody's path is different and pre-determined by The Process. Let go of comparing. It's your ego that compares in a judgmental way. It works on the assumption that you're separate from the person you're comparing yourself with, which is deluded. We're all one. Your true self is that and knows that. We're all doing our bit to contribute towards the overall evolution of The Process. Rejoice and feel inspired when you observe others following The Guidelines.

- **"I'm practicing one guideline, but it's causing me to compromise another. How can I manage that?"** – When guidelines are being practiced correctly, they complement each other rather than compromise each other. I suggest you check to see if you're practicing the guidelines correctly. Try re-reading the chapters relating to the guidelines in question. Also, are you sure the 'compromise' is really a compromise? Sometimes, things we find uncomfortable or unpleasant are actually helping us. Following The Guidelines isn't always a pleasurable experience. Take comfort in the fact that over the long term the fruits of your practice will be more peace and joy.

- "I'm applying The Guidelines as this book suggests, but I'm starting to feel depressed. Am I doing something wrong?" – This may mean that you're trying to do too much, too soon. Slow down your practice. Work with fewer changes or select things that will be easier to change. Paradoxically, through slowing down or doing less, you often make more progress quicker. You have your whole life and beyond to practice.

- "My life was more pleasurable before I started applying The Guidelines. I'm more peaceful now, but I feel like I'm missing out in life" – It's your ego that feels like it's missing out. If your mind is more peaceful, you're experiencing *real life* more of the time. I recommend you take the path of peace rather than the path of pleasure. If you're patient and receptive, The Process will give you all the pleasure that you need. The path of peace contains pleasure. And when it arrives, you can be grateful and enjoy it without attachment.

- "Following The Guidelines is causing me to experience emotional pain. Is this normal and helpful?" – This is often the case because The Process wants to bring your emotional pain to the surface in order to heal it and help you evolve. Use the guidelines, "Be present, bringing awareness and acceptance into every moment" and, "Act with kindness, considering everyone and everything" to help you heal. If the emotional pain is sustained or unbearable then review easing off your practice a little, or seek help from a professional like a doctor or therapist.

- "I'm making some changes to my life so that I can be more aligned with The Guidelines. However, it appears to be causing problems for some people who I love dearly. How should I deal with that?" – Firstly, let me tell you that this is very common when you're on the spiritual path. If you're following The Guidelines properly, and it's always worth checking that you are, it will not be the people you mention that have the problems – it will be their egos. The issue will be that you're changing things that threaten what these people are identified with. It can be related to all sorts of things including belongings, relationships, responsibilities or people feeling exposed in some way by the truth. This will sometimes mean changing or letting go of certain relationships. If you can, be kind and creative. Find ways of following The Guidelines whilst considering others. Never take responsibility for another's suffering; that's their responsibility. Also keep in mind that it's inevitable that people do suffer, even when positive changes are being made around them. People learn and evolve through their suffering. Especially when they're not being guided by spiritual teachings.

- "There are some people that I know who will really benefit from The Guidelines. I can't wait to tell them how they can make their life better! Don't you think that's fantastic?" – It's wonderful that you're appreciating The Guidelines. Be careful when teaching others. Especially those who are close to you like a partner or close family members. In my experience, I usually find that it's best to give people a teaching only when they ask for one. They'll usually do this via a question or asking for your opinion on something. This relates to the guideline, "Do only what needs to be done."

The link to spiritual awakening

There's a strong link between spiritual awakening, also known as enlightenment, and the teachings within this book. When you're awakened or enlightened, like in the case of the Buddha, two things are evident. Firstly, the mind and body are free from any traces of ego. This means freedom from all psychological identifications and suffering. Secondly, the mind will be consistently present and peaceful, regardless of what's going on externally. A manifestation of this is that all guidelines applicable in any moment will be followed. I appreciate the Buddha didn't need to worry about excessive use of social media or mobile phone addiction. That said, if such things were around at the time, I'm sure he would have applied the guideline relating to digital devices!

Many religions and philosophies including those of Buddhism and Yoga describe the different levels of consciousness that lead to enlightenment. Much of the time, the method recommended for achieving higher levels of consciousness and ultimately awakening, is meditation. Whether it's actually possible for a human to become fully awakened or enlightened is beyond my comprehension. I can't prove it either way and keep an open mind. What I do know is that if it is possible, working with

The Guidelines will move you towards it. This is supported through the connections between The Guidelines and similar lists found in religions and philosophies that promote spiritual awakening. It's also supported by millions of practitioners who have raised their levels of consciousness through integrating these spiritual truths. I've certainly experienced higher states of consciousness since I've been following The Guidelines.

If you already have a practice that's working to an end goal of awakening, the guidance found here will integrate beautifully. In fact, the teachings offered in this book reinforce and complement all existing religions and philosophies that are based on the truth.

POINTS FOR REFLECTION

1. Tread your own path and respect that everybody's practice and progress will be different.
2. Change and impermanence makes applying The Guidelines a real-time, lifelong practice.
3. Undertake a practice review regularly and when major life circumstances change.
4. Here are four of the many personal benefits of following The Guidelines:
   a. A peaceful mind.
   b. True enjoyment.
   c. Less suffering.
   d. Better relationships.
5. The above benefits can be used to measure progress.
6. It's best to measure your progress over longer periods of time.
7. To have a rounded practice and to make progress, these three areas need to be considered:
   a. Structured practice.
   b. Everyday activities.
   c. Life conditions.
8. When guidelines are being practiced correctly, they complement each other, rather than compromise each other.
9. Slowing down or doing less often makes your progress quicker.
10. If you're patient and receptive, The Process will give you all the pleasure you need.
11. When you've awakened there will be no traces of ego. The mind will be consistently peaceful and The Guidelines consistently followed.

Afterword

PRACTICING THE TEACHINGS in this book has been incredibly helpful for me. In fact, I would go as far as to say that it's been life changing. It's an honor and a privilege to be able to share them with you. I'm always reassured when I encounter situations in my own life and the lives of others that reaffirm these teachings are spiritually truthful. There's nothing new in the detail of this book. The Guidelines are based on common sense and recommended in teachings from some of the world's great religions and philosophies. There is only one truth. What's new and fresh about this book is the orchestration of these teachings into the seven guidelines. I'm hoping that you find them straightforward to understand and beneficial to apply.

Whilst writing this book, I've often questioned whether I'm credible enough to articulate and spread these wonderful teachings. Mainly because I don't follow them consistently myself; despite trying my best with good intentions. And then I remind myself that I'm a human being treading my own path; changing and evolving, just like everybody else is. Sometimes I'm aligned and peaceful; sometimes I'm misaligned and stressed. The reason I feel good about allowing this book to find its way in the world with my name on the cover, is because I know that I've been present and aligned at the times when I've been writing it. I'm confident that what I've presented to you here is pure and truthful.

Finally, I'd like to wish you all the very best with your practice. I hope that through understanding The Process, and applying The Guidelines, you enjoy an abundance of peace and joy.

> Living by The Guidelines within The Process, is living a life of harmony.

Notes

1. Eckhart Tolle. *The Power of Now: A Guide to Spiritual Enlightenment* (California: New World Library, 2004), Kindle edition.
2. Darren Cockburn. *Being Present: Cultivate a Peaceful Mind through Spiritual Practice*. Vermont: Findhorn Press, 2018.
3. Sri Swami Satchidananda. *Yoga Sutras of Patanjali*. Virginia: Integral Yoga Publications, 2012.
4. Juan Mascaró. *The Upanishads*. Middlesex: Penguin Books, 1965.
5. "Definition of Honour," English Oxford Living Dictionaries, accessed July 12, 2018, https://en.oxforddictionaries.com/definition/honor.
6. Swami Satyananda Saraswati. *Yoga Nidra*. Bihar: Yoga Publications Trust, 2012.
7. "10 things to know about sleep as the clocks change," BBC Website, accessed July 12, 2018, http://www.bbc.co.uk/news/health-41666563.
8. "NHS Choices - Exercise," NHS Website, accessed July 12, 2018, https://www.nhs.uk/Livewell/fitness/Pages/physical-activity-guidelines-for-adults.aspx.
9. Taylor, Steve. *The Leap: The Psychology of Spiritual Awakening (An Eckhart Tolle Edition)* (London: Hay House UK Ltd, 2017), Kindle edition.
10. "Sharon Salzberg Home Page," Sharon Salzberg, accessed July 12, 2018, http://www.sharonsalzberg.com.

Bibliography

"Access to Insight – Readings in Theravāda Buddhism," http://www.accesstoinsight.org.

Burch, Vidyamala, and Danny Penman. *Mindfulness for Health: A practical guide to relieving pain, reducing stress and restoring wellbeing.* London: Piatkus, 2013.

Carrera, Jaganath. *Inside the Yoga Sutras: A comprehensive sourcebook for the study and practice of Patanjali's Yoga Sutras.* Virginia: Integral Yoga Publications, 2006, Kindle edition.

"Eckhart Tolle Now," http://www.eckharttollenow.com.

Moors, Frans. *Liberating Isolation – The Yogasutra of Patanjali.* Chennai: Media Garuda: Krishnamacharya Healing & Yoga Foundation, 2012.

Sri Swami Satchidananda. *Yoga Sutras of Patanjali.* Virginia: Integral Yoga Publications, 2012.

Sutton, Nicholas. *Bhagavad-Gita.* Oxford: The Oxford Centre for Hindu Studies, 2014.

Tolle, Eckhart. *A New Earth: Create a Better Life.* London: Penguin, 2009, Kindle edition.

Williams, Mark, and Danny Penman. *Mindfulness: A practical guide to finding peace in a frantic world.* London: Piatkus, 2011.

About the Author

Photo by John Haworth

DARREN COCKBURN has been practicing meditation and mindfulness for over twenty years, studying with a range of teachers from different religions. As a coach and teacher, he's supported hundreds of people in meditation, mindfulness, and finding a connection to spirituality. His focus is on applying spiritual teachings in everyday life to cultivate a peaceful mind.

Outside of his work, the author of *Being Present* and *Living a Life of Harmony* enjoys reading, walking in nature, spending time with friends and his two children. In addition, he is very passionate about yoga.

For more information on Darren please visit: **www.darrencockburn.com**

Also by this Author

Being Present
by Darren Cockburn

PROVIDING INSIGHT into how to cultivate a peaceful mind through the power of the present moment, Darren Cockburn shares practical exercises, meditations, and supportive wisdom teachings centered on mindfulness, breath, and immersion in nature to simplify your life, free yourself from unhelpful thought patterns, and have a calmer, more connected experience of life.

Alongside an introduction to meditation techniques and supportive wisdom teachings from Buddhist and other spiritual traditions, Darren provides useful guidance on successfully integrating a regular spiritual practice into your day-to-day activities. He also includes pointers on how to create your own unique and personal structure in order to support your ongoing spiritual practice, the fruits of which will ultimately be a peaceful, calmer, and more connected experience of life.

978-1-84409-746-3